WHAT LIES BEHIND THE PICTURE?

A Personal Journey into Cree Ancestry

Vernon R. Wishart

Editing and Foreword
by
Linda Goyette

Copyright © 2006 Vernon R. Wishart

All rights reserved. No part of this book may be reproduced by any means, electronic or mechanical, including photography, recording, or any information and retrieval system, without the prior written permission of the Publisher, or in the case of photocopying or other reprographic copying, a license from CANCOPY (Canadian Copyright Licensing Agency), 1 Yonge Street, Suite 1900, Toronto ON M5E 1E5, fax (416) 868-1621.

Credits
Cover and text design by Full Court Press
Printed and bound in Canada

Library and Archives Canada Cataloguing in Publication
Wishart, Vernon R. (Vernon Roy), 1927–
What lies behind the picture? : a personal journey into Cree ancestry / Vernon R. Wishart.
Includes bibliographical references and index.
ISBN 0-929123-14-X
1. Wishart, Vernon R. (Vernon Roy), 1927– —Family. 2. Cree, Indians—Northwest, Canadian—Biography. 3. Northwest, Canadian—History. I. Central Alberta Historical Society II. Title.
E99.C88W57   2006   971.2'00497323'00922   C2006-901029-3

CONTENTS

Foreword 7

—PROLOGUE—
What Lies Behind the Picture? *13*

—FIRST ENCOUNTERS—
CHAPTER 1
Isaac Batt and his Cree Wife *30*
CHAPTER 2
Nestichio Batt and James Spence *42*

—WILLIAM FLETT AND SASKATCHEWAN—
CHAPTER 3
A Country Marriage *56*
CHAPTER 4
Flett's Journal at Edmonton House *69*
CHAPTER 5
Saskatchewan: A Venerable Sojourner *76*
CHAPTER 6
Journey into the Unknown *86*

—THE WISHARTS—
CHAPTER 7
Thomas Wishart: Adventure by Sea *102*
CHAPTER 8
Journey Inland *108*
CHAPTER 9
Thomas and Barbara *114*

—JAMES AND ELIZA—
CHAPTER 10
Eliza's Medicine Bag *124*

CHAPTER 11
The Trek West and the Métis Struggle *134*
CHAPTER 12
Prairie Fires *145*
CHAPTER 13
Aftermath of the Rebellion *155*
CHAPTER 14
Journey to the Promised Land *160*

—LOOKING BACK—
CHAPTER 15
They Are Remembered *164*
CHAPTER 16
My Personal Journey *172*

—EPILOGUE—
Defining Moments *181*

Acknowledgements 183
Notes 185
Bibliography 211
Index 219
About the Author 232

To my sister Shirley Wishart, who started me on this journey of discovery. Without her research, inspiration and guidance this book would not have been possible.

Foreword

EVERY FAMILY IS A MYSTERY. WE OWE OUR EXISTENCE TO great-great-great grandparents, and to the generations that stand in the shadows behind them, yet these ancestors are strangers to us. They gave us our family names, our genetic inheritance, our breath, and yet we know nothing of their joys and sorrows, secrets and fears, struggles and triumphs. Their life stories are locked boxes in the world's attic, and we have lost the key.

How many of us look over our shoulders for a glimpse of the strangers in the shadows? Some inquisitive people will search for a family photograph album, a love letter, a baptismal certificate, a land title document, a faded quilt or an old saddle, as a way to touch the lives of ancestors: to prove they lived, to prove they mattered. This detective work is difficult, a hunt in the dark. Few people bother.

Vern Wishart is a more determined man. This thoughtful Albertan is blessed with the twin gifts of curiosity and persistence. Tell him a story, and he'll ask another question. Vern stumbled upon the secret of his Cree ancestry by accident, and intrigued, he began a long quest through the historical records of western Canada for the complicated truth about his family. He wanted to

What Lies Behind the Picture?

do more than collect birth dates and death dates for a genealogical chart, checking off each name as a kind of conquest. He wanted more precise information than historians could provide in their books and scholarly articles. Vern was looking for vivid, personal stories. He searched for the key to the locked box until he found it.

Two clues inspired his quest: a story about his great-grandmother's medicine bag, and a snapshot of his father holding him when he was a baby.

Vern crisscrossed western Canada and travelled to Orkney and the United States in a decade of historical sleuthing. He and his sister, Shirley Wishart, examined the journals, letters and business records of the Hudson's Bay Company, and the genealogical records and travel narratives of the early West. They checked informal family stories against the historical record with laborious research.

In the pages of *What Lies Behind the Picture?*, Vern introduces some unforgettable people. A Cree woman named Saskatchewan raises a family with the Orcadian fur trader William Flett at Fort Edmonton, and later accompanies her young grandchildren on a dangerous journey over the mountains to Oregon in 1841. Trader Isaac Batt is murdered for his bad judgement; his daughter Nestichio survives him to begin a Canadian family with her father's friend, James Spence. Thomas Wishart confronts icebergs on the stormy Atlantic with the doomed explorer Sir John Franklin. Dislocated by the disappearance of the buffalo, and the Métis and Cree rebellions, Eliza and James Wishart search for land they can call their own, and finally find a haven called Rosebud. After a prairie blizzard Eliza saves her husband's life when she chops off his frozen toes with a butcher knife, and treats his wounds with the traditional remedies of her ancestors.

Adventure stories are irresistible, but the personal honesty in this book is what makes it exceptional. In his journey toward his father's secret, Vern discovers the price his family members paid for their interracial ancestry in the tense years after the Red River Resistance of 1870 and the North-West Rebellion of 1885. He investigates the racism in the contemporary West that too often confines unnamed aboriginal people to the first vague chapters

Foreword

of history books, and to the margins of public consciousness. He names and honours the aboriginal grandmothers of the territory, and their descendants. Through sensitive storytelling, the author challenges westerners of all backgrounds to consider one another as possible relatives, and not antagonistic strangers.

How many Canadian families are like the Fletts, the Spences and the Wisharts? Hundreds of thousands, I suspect. Members of the same extended family can live on opposite sides of a racial divide—some identifying themselves as aboriginal, some as Euro-Canadian—yet all with the same surname and the same great-great grandparents.

Many western Canadians have a vague knowledge of their Cree, Blackfoot, Métis, Mixed-Blood, Québecois, English and Orkney Islands ancestry, but no concept of the rich and difficult lives of family members who worked in the early fur trade. Older people with mixed ancestry say with some embarrassment that their parents or grandparents identified themselves as French-Canadian or Scottish to avoid ostracism and racism in a hostile atmosphere between 1885 and about 1970. Today younger people can ask for family stories at the kitchen table, and hear nothing that satisfies their curiosity because their parents have no information.

Yet for all the barriers, a door is opening. Statistics Canada demographers report that the significant rise in Canada's identified aboriginal population in the last decade is not a simple matter of rising birth rates. An increasing number of Canadians are identifying themselves as Métis or First Nations members after vigorous genealogical research. These Canadians are not always content with a letter from a genealogist, a treaty number or a Metis Nation card. They are searching for personal identity and meaning, for new understanding in divided communities, and for the satisfying story behind a blurry and confusing picture.

Vern Wishart captures the essence of that quest in his writing. His book is a bold step in the direction of reconciliation in western Canada, and a beautiful family reunion.

–Linda Goyette

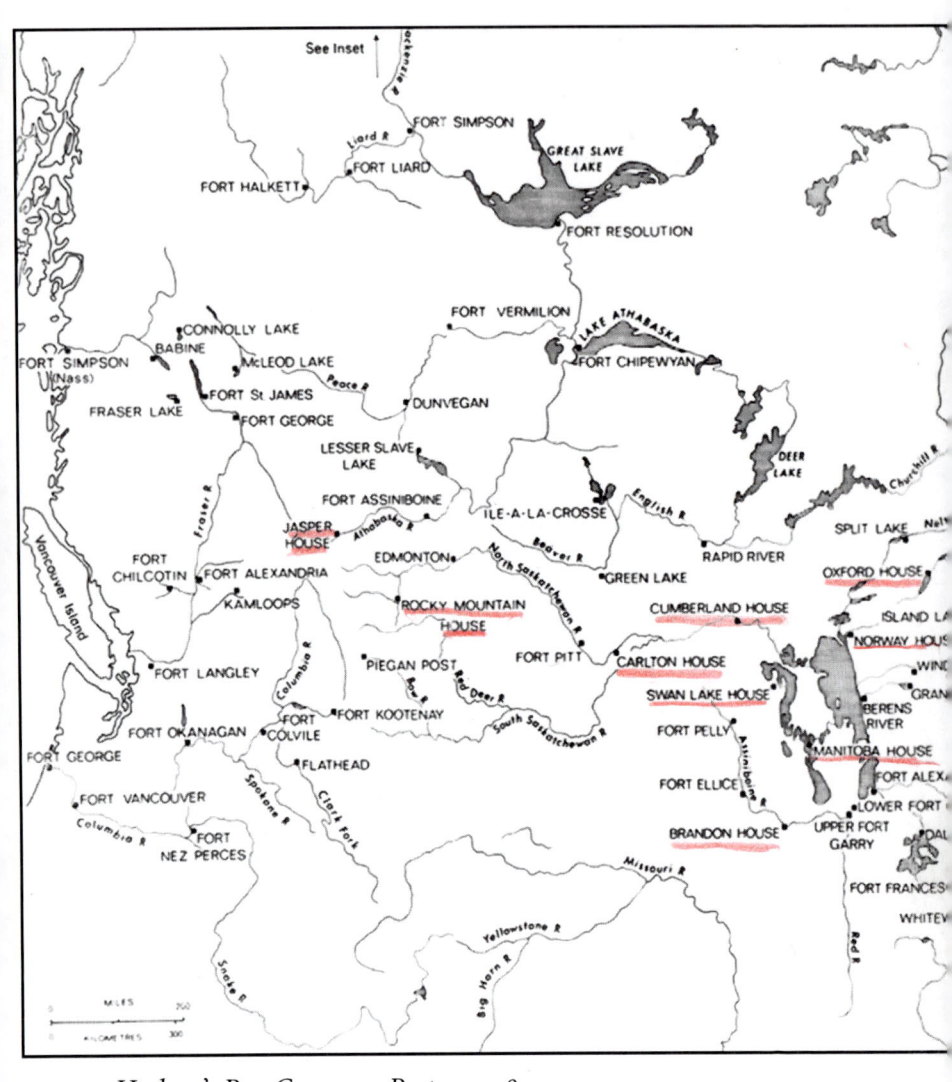

Hudson's Bay Company Posts, ca. 1832
HUDSON'S BAY COMPANY ARCHIVES

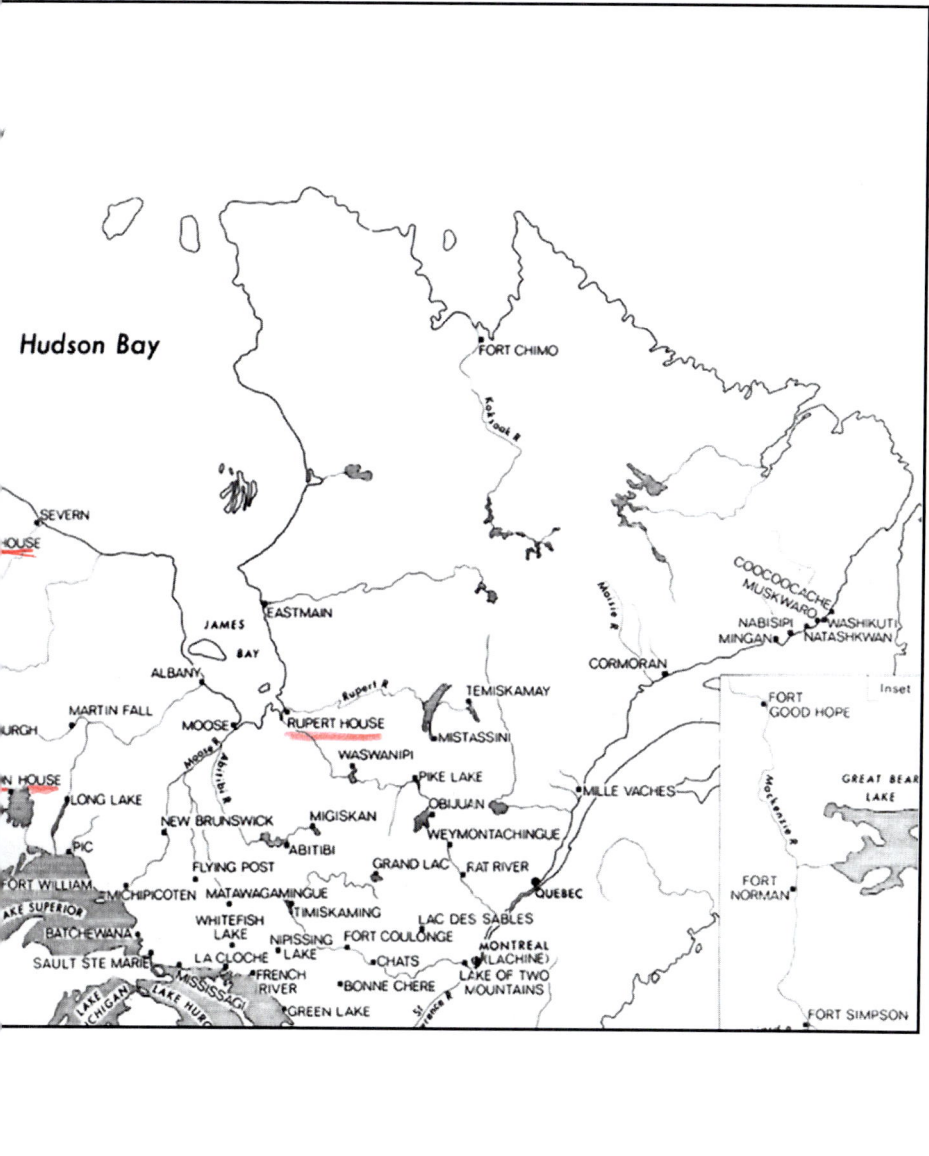

*The lines have fallen for me in pleasant places;
yea, I have a goodly heritage.*
Psalm 16:6

PROLOGUE

What Lies Behind the Picture?

I HOLD A TREASURED PHOTOGRAPH IN MY HANDS, LOOKING at my father's face in the shadows, wondering about him. Turning over the snapshot, I can read my mother's handwriting on the back: "Roy and Vern at Morningside—Vern two weeks old, nineteen twenty-seven."

In the picture I am wrapped in a blanket. On my head is a knitted bonnet. It extends around my ears and under my chin. In my mouth is a baby's pacifier. I am looking at my father, whom I was never able to bring into complete focus until years after his death. The reason is that he held within him a secret he carried to his grave, something he did not want to reveal and did everything to conceal. If Mother knew, she kept it from us. It was sealed from view until, quite by chance, the seal was broken, thus opening up for me a deeper understanding of my father and a new sense of my own identity.

My father is dressed in working clothes, a loose-fitting shirt and pants that have been soiled by a particular kind of work. Dad was a grain buyer, a high priest in one of those many sentinels that once dotted the prairie landscape, the grain elevator.

What Lies Behind the Picture?

My father and I, 1927
AULTA WISHART

Prologue

Artist A. Y. Jackson, of the Group of Seven, came west to paint and fell in love with these simply crafted towering structures. He called them "cathedrals" and wrote, "Like France's cathedrals, the prairies have their grain elevators, white and silver and red—I think they are lovely things."[1] I don't think A. Y. was ever inside an elevator or he might have come up with another name. Even on a warm day, its barn-like interior, designed for receiving and storing grain carried by wagon or truck, was drafty. Grain dust permeated every nook and cranny. The powdery particles, combined with my father's habit of smoking, likely contributed to the lung cancer that caused his death when he was only 54.

I was allergic to grain dust, and though I often helped Dad at the elevator, I inevitably ended up with a congested chest, irritated skin and watering eyes. My calling was not to be a high priest in one of the cathedrals that interrupted the prairie landscape. It would be a calling of a different nature. I became a minister of the United Church of Canada.

The hands that hold me in the photo are large hands—the hands of a labourer. And yet, there are parts of the attire that say, *I am something more.* On my father's head is a hat with a wide band. There are armbands keeping the shirt sleeves neatly tucked and the cuffs in place. In later years, as a successful grain buyer and travelling superintendent with a territory encompassing many prairie elevators, he would come to wear a carefully pressed shirt, trousers, jacket and a tie.

It is the head and face of my father that capture my attention. The head is large and handsome, the complexion tanned. The mouth is firm. The eyes? They are partially hidden by the shadow of the hat, but they are dark and reflective. Is he contemplating what the future holds for the child in his arms if his secret should become known?

Six years after our father's death in 1959, my sister Shirley was attending a shower for a friend in Calgary, Alberta. Someone present asked if she knew a John Martin, who lived in a small town northeast of Calgary called Rosebud. He had written a book of local history in which he talked about the Wisharts. Apparently, he was a self-educated man with an eye and ear for

What Lies Behind the Picture?

history. Shirley arranged a visit with John Martin. My sister was given a copy of *The Rosebud Trail*, which contained the story of the Great Blizzard of 1887, a prairie snowstorm which brought the spectre of death perilously close to the homestead of our great-grandparents, James and Eliza Wishart.[2]

As children, we never enquired about our father's grandparents, and information was never volunteered. The bits of information we happened to gather did not quicken our interest or curiosity. A curtain was quietly drawn around James and Eliza. Now the curtain opened and they emerged from the past onto the horizon of our lives in the account of The Great Blizzard.

I have followed Martin's account of the blizzard, as well as that of Mary Cook, James and Eliza's daughter, in my retelling of the events as they relate to James and Eliza.[3] The story in brief is this:

James Wishart, in order to obtain much-needed supplies, hooked up his team of horses, John and Grey, to a sleigh and set out to Gleichen some 50 kilometres away. While in Gleichen, which is about 65 kilometres east southeast of Calgary, he picked up his mail and supplies at Vic Beaupre's store and was about to leave when Crane Bear, a Blackfoot Native, said, "Do not go! A bad storm is on its way."[4] Jim was no stranger to winter storms. Besides, he was warmly clad in a buffalo coat and cap, wool mitts, badger skin gauntlets, and moose hide moccasins. Disregarding Crane Bear's warning, he wrapped himself in his buffalo robes and headed his team for home.

Before he had travelled many kilometres, fast-moving clouds rolled ominously overhead. In the distance a solid bank of snow was fast approaching. *It's just a flurry,* Jim told himself. By the time he reached Chimney Hill some 15 kilometres from home, visibility was zero. Sky and snow had become one. Indeed, the storm was so severe that further travel was out of the question. Jim drove his team into a coulee on the west side of the hill, and dug into a snowbank under a sandstone ledge, known today as Chimney Rock. He covered old John with a tarp and tied him to the sleigh, hoping he could ride him home after the storm subsided. Grey, he turned loose.[5]

Prologue

James and Eliza Wishart
SHIRLEY WISHART

He spent the next two days and nights living on flour and snow. Every few hours, when the snowbank at the mouth of the cave became heavy and threatened to become an icy tomb, he cleared away an opening. By the morning of the third day, the storm had passed into Montana leaving in its wake many settlers frozen to death in their flimsy shacks. Thousands of cattle were trapped and frozen in banks of snow, as was faithful Grey.[6] The bitter cold had taken its toll on Jim. His hands and feet were

What Lies Behind the Picture?

frostbitten. To make matters worse, his horse, John, was frozen solid right where he had been tied. Jim's situation was precarious. If he was to survive, he had to walk the remaining 15 kilometres to reach home. He set out, his six-foot-six frame plunging through snow that often came to his waist. His rapid breath left a vapour trail and frozen icicles on his beard. When his legs failed to carry him any longer over the huge drifts, he collapsed.

As Jim lay in the snow prepared to die, he heard a voice say, *Jim! Get up Jim, and have one more try.*[7]

He staggered to his feet and fell. He began crawling on his hands and knees, clawing his way forward. Slowly and desperately he dragged his body, now numbed by cold, through the snow. Just as night was settling, he topped the hill which stood a few hundred metres from his home, and then fell forward in a heap, totally and utterly exhausted.

Eliza had been watching for him at the window of their log cabin. She hoped that her husband had waited out the storm in Gleichen. Noticing a dark object in the snow, she called their son, Dave. The two of them went out into the night; Mary and Herb, the younger children, remained in the cabin. Dave took his rifle thinking it might be a bear. Suddenly, they realized it was a human form. It was Jim!

They half-dragged and half-carried Jim's large, partially frozen frame back to the house. Warm blankets, hot tea and soup gradually revived the bone-cold traveller. The extent of the damage to his body was soon determined. Jim's frostbitten fingers and toes were in bad shape. Miraculously, his fingers did not turn gangrenous, but his toes did. The tall, rugged husband and petite, comely wife clasped hands and resolutely looked into each other's eyes. They both knew that if Jim was to live the toes had to be amputated.

Eliza moved swiftly. She carefully placed one of Jim's affected feet on a block of wood. While Dave held his father's shoulders, she held a butcher knife on the joint below the gangrene of the big toe and carefully raised and struck the knife with a hammer. With the crunch of sinew and the gush of blood, Eliza grew pale. She moved the knife to the next toe. Once again the primitive opera-

Prologue

James Wishart
SHIRLEY WISHART

tion was repeated. Perspiration poured from Jim's face, which was now contorted in pain. Eliza moved the blood-splattered blade to the next toe. Severed toe and blood spurted forth. Eliza fainted.

While Dave knelt and attended to his mother, Jim, though dazed from the ordeal, picked the bloody knife up from the floor, held it to his remaining toes and raised the hammer once again, and again, until the torturous amputations were completed. As Jim sank to the floor, Eliza revived.

The story then comes to the source of my father's secret and hidden pain. I quote directly from the account: "Eliza's knowledge of Indian medicine and surgery saved Jim's life."[8] These words were our first indication that our great-grandparents were of Mixed-blood.

In those strokes of hammer on flesh, sinew and bone, our roots were laid bare.

Our father, while not knowing the full story of his origins, could not escape the fact of his Mixed-blood background. Shirley discovered in a conversation with a family member that when Dad's mother, Maude, and his father, Dave, argued, she often called him "Half-breed."[9] She did not mean it in a kindly way. Within the environs of his own home, Dad very likely came to believe, at an early age, that a Native heritage was not something of which to be proud. As a boy, he was very probably taunted by peers who called him "Half-breed." It is possible that his Native heritage meant little to him and he was simply

with an insult

> The Cree described people of Native-European origin as *ápihtawikosán*. Historically the word *Half-breed* was not pejorative but became increasingly so over time and is no longer used. The French word *Métis* is not pejorative and is properly used to describe descendants of Native and French marriages in Western Canada. I will use the historic term *Mixed-blood* to refer to the descendants of Scottish, mainly Orkney men, or Englishmen and their Native wives in the North West.[10]

Prologue

unconcerned about his family roots and racial identity. The weight of evidence, however, is that his Mixed-blood heritage was something he wished to hide.

Dave and Maude moved, with their family, from the Rosebud area to Gleichen. Dad recalled, during his boyhood in Gleichen, how he joined with others in chasing Blackfoot boys across the tracks back to their reserve. In that racist act was he seeking to dissociate himself from his Native background?

Many years after our father's death, we were visiting our mother, who was in the Foothills Hospital, in Calgary, Alberta. The woman who shared the room with Mother was from Gleichen. Shirley overheard her saying to a friend, in a loud whisper, "They are Wisharts, Half-breeds you know."

The woman's comments confirmed our belief that Dad had grown up in an environment in which he experienced racism and painful discrimination. In that time, and in the circles in which he spent his youth, many thought having "Indian blood" was something of which to be ashamed. Our father likely determined very early that he did not want his children to experience what he had faced. He hoped to give us a fair opportunity as we made our way in the world.

The secret that lies within the photograph of my father and me is our Native roots. This photo has become one of my most cherished possessions. In the recesses of my father's eyes I see the hope that the knowledge of those roots would go to the grave with him. He never lived long enough for us to lift that burden from him. By tracing our ancestry and telling the whole story, we can say to all what we never had the opportunity to say to our father:

Dad, we are tremendously proud of the fact that in our family tree we have Native ancestry, that we have a link with the Aboriginal people, a people who were inhabitants of this land for thousands of years before the white man came. We are tremendously proud of the Native women in our background, without whom our ancestors, as rugged as they were, would have been unable to survive and thrive. We are proud of James and Eliza, of who they were and what they did, and we are proud of you.

What Lies Behind the Picture?

My story of our family's roots relies heavily on the extensive research done by my sister Shirley. She spent weeks delving into the Hudson's Bay Company Archives housed in the Archives of Manitoba in Winnipeg, and the Glenbow Museum in Calgary, Alberta. As well, she visited relatives in Montana and Manitoba. She wrote letters, interviewed people, taped conversations, took notes, collected photographs and charted genealogies. In 1992, she went to Orkney, Scotland, to attend the Centre for Rupert's Land Studies Colloquium. While there she was able to do further research and had the pleasure of meeting relatives who also traced their roots to the Hudson's Bay Company. In 1993, she organized a reunion in Elk Point, Alberta, of the Batt, Spence, Flett, Halcro and Wishart fur trade descendants. Those who accepted the invitation to trace their lineage and honour their Native roots numbered in the fifties and came from as far east as Manitoba and as far west as British Columbia.

Shortly before my retirement, Shirley and I together hiked the Wishart Trail named after James and Eliza, which is located in the Gaetz Lake Sanctuary in Red Deer, Alberta. It was as though we were walking back in time, for above the trail was the site of their log cabin; below the trail were the two small lakes where Dave, our grandfather, as a young man trapped muskrats and his sisters gathered mud hens' eggs for cooking. From that moment on my interest in our Native heritage began to take flight.

Since retiring from the ministry in 1993, I have been able, with Shirley's encouragement and guidance, to pick up her research and flesh it out with new sources and added information. Shirley, meanwhile, is in the process of gathering material from her extensive files. While her writing hand still suffers from the effects of a stroke, she has been able to resume this work. Her finished manuscript will be more comprehensive and have a different focus and style from mine.

Our family is strong on family gatherings in which stories are told and retold. The oral tradition is alive and well in these get-togethers. We have been, until recently, weak in our knowl-

Prologue

edge of the past. What follows is an attempt to look into the past in order to reveal something of our family's roots. As we reconstruct the past, we are fortunate that documentation is accessible. Historical events supply the background for organizing the material. In some instances, I have tried to fill in the spaces where no first-hand information is known or likely to be known.

This undertaking arises from the conviction that only in understanding our origin as families and as individuals can we move with sureness into the future. Where we are now, and where we are going, is related in important ways to the past. The men and women you will meet in these pages continue to influence our lives and our perceptions.

As you travel with me in this exploration of my family roots, you will discover the story of ordinary people who witnessed the early history of Western Canada. It is a story that until recently remained hidden because racial prejudice encouraged our father to hide his Native ancestry as a survival strategy.

OUR LINEAGE

AS THE READER FOLLOWS THIS HISTORICAL NARRATIVE, IT may be difficult to keep people in their time frame. To assist with dates and relationships, I have provided a genealogical chart. In doing so, I have traced only that lineage which has direct connection with our Native ancestry.

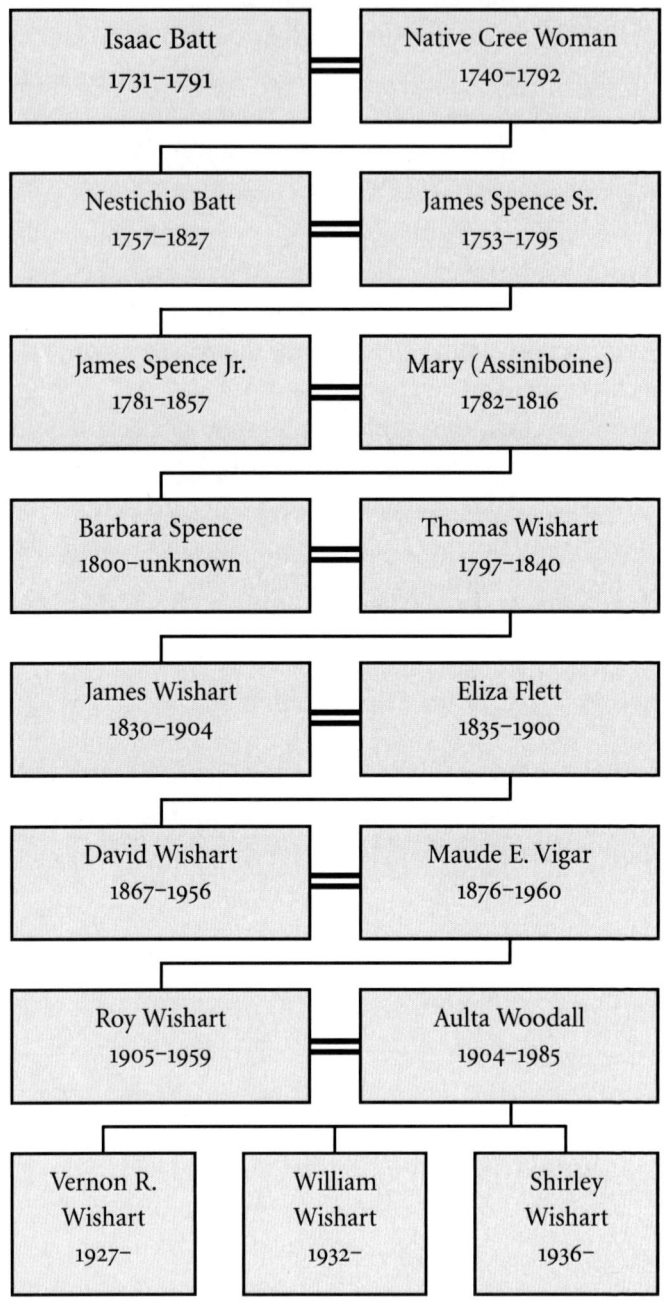

Prologue
DESCENDANTS of WILLIAM FLETT

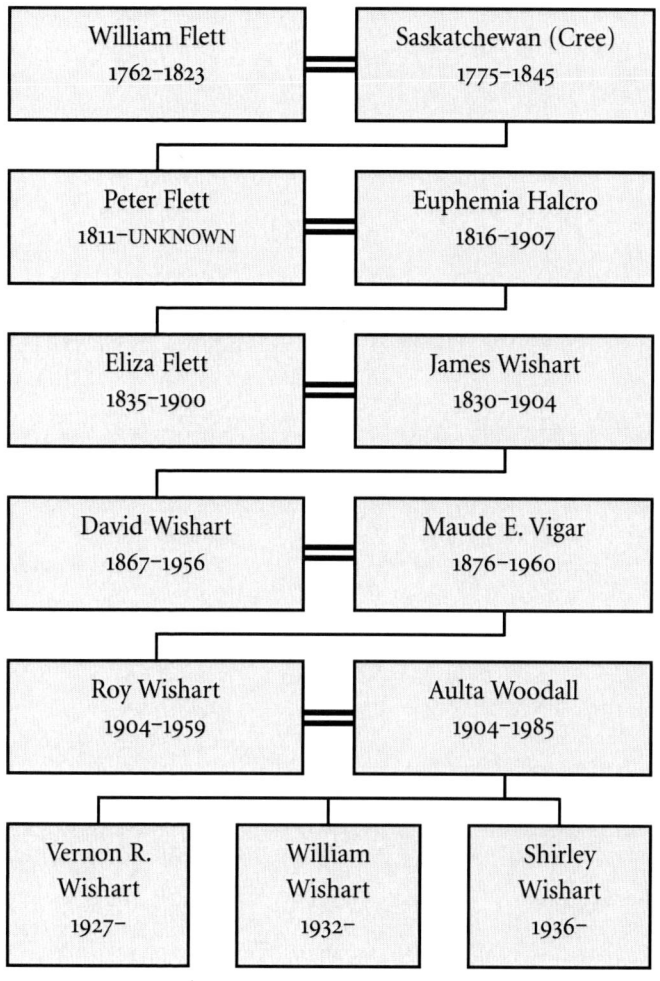

FIRST ENCOUNTERS

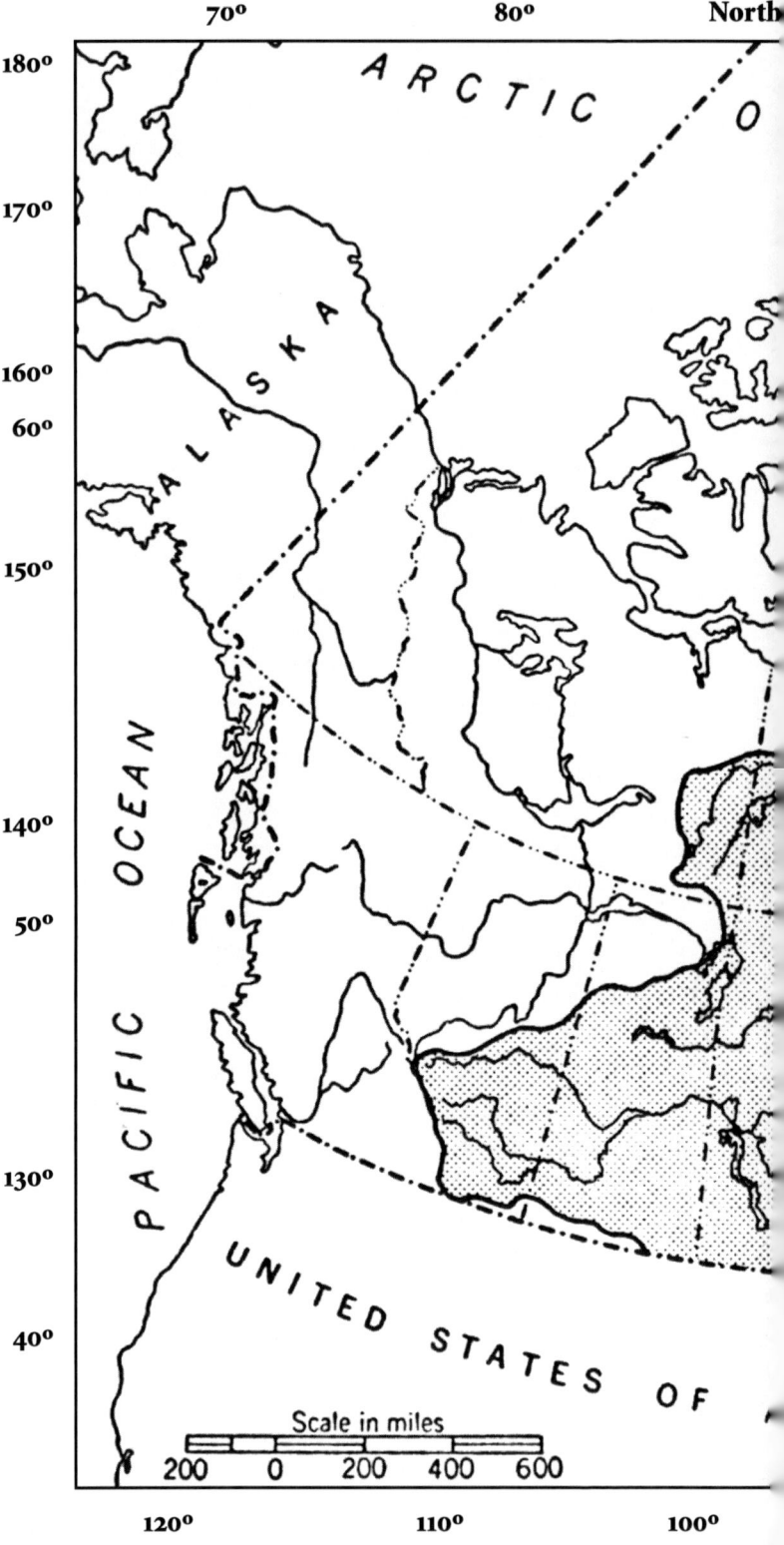

Rupert's Land, after 1818, according to an 1857 map by J. Arrowsmith
MINISTER OF SUPPLY AND SERVICES, CANADA

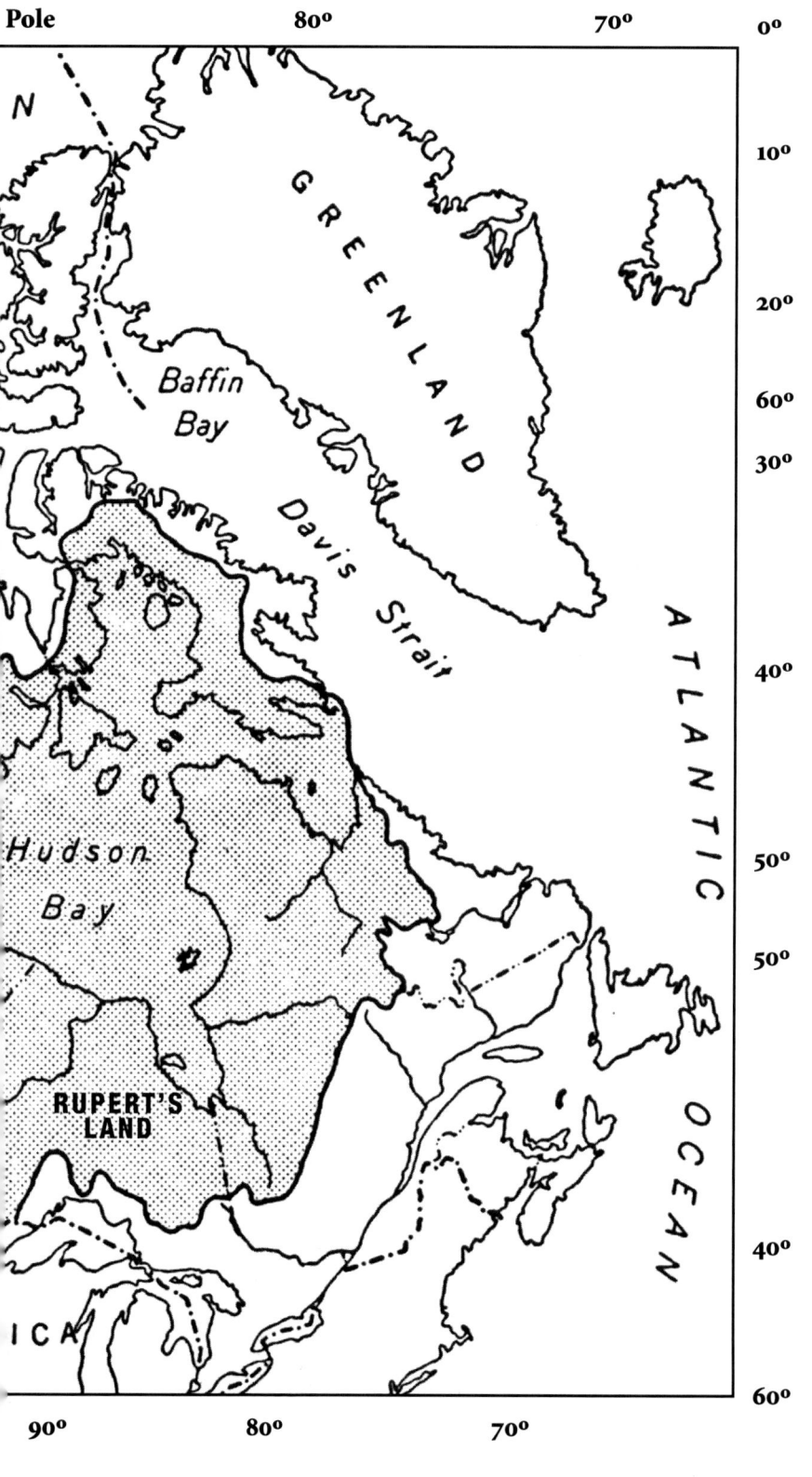

CHAPTER 1

Isaac Batt and His Cree Wife

WHICH TELLS THE STORY OF OUR ANCESTORS, ISAAC BATT, AN ENGLISHMAN, WHO WAS A FUR TRADER WITH THE HUDSON'S BAY COMPANY, AND HIS COUNTRY WIFE, A NATIVE WOMAN WHOSE NAME WE DO NOT KNOW, AND WITH WHOM OUR NATIVE HERITAGE BEGINS.

THE STORY OF OUR NATIVE ROOTS BEGINS WITH A CREE woman who was the country wife of an Englishman named Isaac Batt.[1] Unlike Batt, her name does not appear in the historical records of the day. It is very likely that our Native ancestor was a Swampy Cree which designates the Cree people residing in the marshy lowlands of Hudson and James Bay.[2] They use the term Omushkego to identify themselves which means "People of the muskeg." The Native encampment near York Factory was called the Home Guard, and was likely made up of the Swampy Cree who inhabited the area. It is probable that Batt's Native wife was among the Home Guard, or among the Swampy of that area.

Batt was born about 1731 in Stanstead Abbots, Hertfordshire, England. We know little about him except that in 1754, while in his twenties, he contracted with the Hudson's Bay Company and departed on one of their boats from Gravesend, England, to serve for five years at £10 per year as a labourer at York Factory, on the shores of Hudson Bay, in Rupert's Land.

For almost a century successive generations of my family

Isaac Batt and His Cree Wife

Indian woman and child
HUDSON'S BAY COMPANY ARCHIVES

What Lies Behind the Picture?

would enter the service of this all-powerful fur trading company. The Hudson's Bay Company (HBC) was always more than a business monopoly; it became a corporate autocracy that claimed the sovereign right to rule a vast territory whether the inhabitants approved or not. When King Charles II incorporated the HBC on May 2, 1670, he authorized his cousin Prince Rupert and 17 associates to trade in fur or anything else for profit as "true and absolute Lordes and Proprietors of the same Territory." Rupert's Land was named after Prince Rupert, the Company's first governor. Under the terms of the Charter, this territory spanned the "Seas Streightes Bayes Rivers Lakes Creekes and Soundes" of Hudson Bay's vast drainage network, holding a quarter of the world's fresh surface water—and an estimated ten million beaver. In modern geographical terms it included northern Quebec and Ontario, north of the Laurentian watershed, all of Manitoba, parts of Saskatchewan, Alberta, and a portion of the Northwest Territories and Nunavut.

Isaac Batt joined the host of men who since 1670 had laboured on behalf of the HBC to satisfy Europe's demand for furs, especially the pelt of the beaver. The lustrous coat of this pug-nosed rodent, which haunted the streams and lakes of Rupert's Land, supplied Europe's fashion demands for beaver-felt hats.

Batt adjusted to his new surroundings with unusual speed. He learned quickly the skills required for travel and trade in an environment where true grit was a necessity for survival.

During these years of Batt's service, the French were challenging the HBC monopoly. They had established numerous forts

> The tanned pelt of a prime winter beaver, termed Made Beaver or MB, quickly became the standard of trade for the HBC. All other furs and goods were measured against it. For example, a gun might be traded for 10 MB; a single MB could be traded for a brass kettle or a kilogram of Brazil tobacco.

reaching into the interior as far as Fort á La Corne near the confluence of the North and South Saskatchewan Rivers, close to present-day Prince Albert, Saskatchewan. At these posts, the French intercepted and traded with the Natives on their way downstream to York Factory on Hudson Bay.

York Factory began as a humble fur trading post in 1682. After 40 years of warring with France over control of Hudson Bay, Britain secured York Factory, named for the Duke of York, following the Treaty of Utrecht in 1713. While set in an unattractive and swampy landscape, it was strategically placed on a narrow peninsula between the mouths of the Nelson and Hayes Rivers. The Hayes was the best route inland and connected York to a massive hinterland. It was gradually built into the largest and most profitable Company post and served as the HBC's main trans-shipment post for the next 150 years.

The HBC, in order to counter the French threat, instructed James Isham, who was in charge of York Factory, to obtain better knowledge of the interior. The person chosen to gain this information was Anthony Henday.

In 1754, Henday made an epic journey of 4000 kilometres in 51 weeks. His constant companion was a Cree woman who supplied his food, and acted as his interpreter and "bed-fellow." The purpose of this historic trek was to obtain a better knowledge of the territory outside the confines of York Factory, and to make contact with the Blackfoot in order to encourage them to trade with the HBC. Henday travelled farther into Western Canada than any HBC trader before him. In 1754–55, he went as far west as present-day Antler Hill, north of today's Innisfail, from where he recorded seeing the "shining mountains." He must have been impressed by the Rockies for he visited the hill one last time before he and his party turned eastward. While the Blackfoot extended to him their hospitality, they were unwilling to enter into trading relations. The most valuable information he brought back was that the Cree were so firmly established as the middlemen in the fur trade that they would not allow other Natives to make the long journey to York Factory to trade. During his travels, Henday was impressed with the French

What Lies Behind the Picture?

traders: "The French talk several languages to perfection; they have the advantage of us in every shape, and if they had Brazile tobacco would entirely cut our trade off."[3]

Henday's report prompted the HBC to begin making plans to safeguard its fur trade by establishing posts in the interior. The plans were not acted upon. Decisive events were transpiring which would shape the future of Western Canada. The 150-year struggle between the French and the English for North America ended with Wolfe's victory on the Plains of Abraham, Quebec, in 1759. There followed the Treaty of Paris in 1763 in which France ceded to Britain all her claims and possessions in North America. Canada became a British colony and the French traders were forced to withdraw.

It was during the period of inland exploration and intense rivalry with the French traders, before their withdrawal in 1763, that Isaac Batt joined the service of the HBC.

In July 1758, Batt left York Factory on a journey inland for the purpose of encouraging Native people to bring their trade to York Factory. He returned to York in June 1759, but almost immediately set out again for the interior, returning in June 1760. The HBC had good reason for sending Batt inland. In a letter dated 29 August, 1759, to the Governor and Committee in London, James Isham, the Chief Factor at York Factory, writes, "Isaac Batt who arrived at the head of 64 canoes last June, is again returned inland."[4] What an encouraging sight that must have been to Isham—Isaac Batt in a flotilla of fur-laden canoes! Little wonder it was profitable to send men like Batt inland from York Factory. Within six years of his arrival, he had become an experienced inland traveller and trader. Relying on the guidance and experience of Natives,[5] he travelled tremendous distances inland, wintering with Native people.

> While the HBC officially prohibited its men from taking Native wives, as early as 1740 journal entries acknowledged marital relationships with Native women.[6]

Isaac Batt and His Cree Wife

In the autumn of 1760, he returned to England, and in April 1761 the Governor and Committee of the HBC granted him a gift of money:

> . . . in consideration of having Travelled two Years inland among the Natives in Hudson's Bay for the Advancement of their [the Company's] Trade, and for his extraordinary pains and Labour therein, as well as for a recompence for the dangers and difficulty Attending the same.[7]

While in England, Batt married Sarah Fowler. In the spring of 1762, however, he was re-engaged by the Company, and proceeded once again to York Factory. Sarah did not accompany him. Company policy, which emphasized fur trading rather than colonization, initially barred the presence of white women in the land claimed by the HBC.

It is likely that at this point Batt decided his life would be spent in the service of the HBC. There was another reason he turned his back on England and his bride. Before he married Sarah, Batt already had a wife and family in Rupert's Land; he had taken a Cree woman for his wife very soon after his arrival in 1754. Batt, by his Native wife, had a daughter named Nestichio, who was born about 1757. Like many other traders, he had a wife in the Old Country and one in the New. During the years 1763–66, Batt had £4 to £5 deducted annually from his wages for the support of his wife who remained in England; but we hear no more of Sarah after 1766.

Batt's knowledge of Native ways indicates an early and constant tutor in the ways of the land. Whether Isaac Batt's union with a Native woman was to secure a trading advantage for the HBC, or for his own purposes, we will never know. One thing is certain: his wife's knowledge of what was necessary to survive in an often harsh environment would be a large factor in enabling Batt to travel inland. On 13 May, 1763 London wrote, "Therefore we again direct that some of our servants, particularly Isaac Batt whose ability we thereto have experienced and any other that can be depended upon to go inland to get natives to bring furs to York."[8]

From 1763 until 1774, with the exception of 1772, he went inland in each successive trading season.[9] Young Nestichio accompanied her parents on many of these journeys.[10]

What Lies Behind the Picture?

Anthony Henday's journal mentions that Isaac Batt, along with other notable inland traders, greatly increased the immediate fur returns at York Factory. Henday also notes their contribution to the Company's knowledge of the lands it claimed and the people who inhabited them.

We know little of Batt's wife, who is one link to our Native heritage, except for an entry in Samuel Hearne's Journals. Hearne, who also had a Native wife, entered the HBC employ in 1766 and was chosen to search for a western passage to the Arctic and possible trading routes. He followed the Coppermine River to the Arctic Ocean but realized it was of little material advantage to the HBC. In his book *Journey to the Northern Ocean,* Samuel Hearne left this rather unflattering account of Isaac Batt:

It is common for the Southern Indians to tame and domesticate the young cubs, and they are frequently taken so young that they cannot eat. On those occasions, the Indians oblige their wives who have milk in their breast to suckle them. And one of the Company's servants whose name is Isaac Batt, willing to be as great a brute as his Indian companions, absolutely forced one of his wives who had recently lost her infant, to suckle a young bear.[11]

While this was upsetting to Hearne, who seemed to condemn Batt for this incident, it was likely not so upsetting to Batt who was acquainted with Native ways. Apparently it was not an uncommon practice, after the death of a baby, for the mother to relieve engorged breasts by means of an orphaned bear cub. Among many Native people, the bear was viewed as the most intelligent of animals, sometimes referred to as "half human" and having spiritual powers.[12] "Hearne may have been unaware of these views of the power and importance of bears, and perhaps Isaac Batt knew more of Cree ways than his celebrated superior."[13]

Our first Native ancestor remains hidden in the pages of time, aside from this one recorded event by Samuel Hearne. Even this early record may not refer to our ancestor, given the fact that Hearne writes that Batt had more than one wife. Likely Batt followed the pattern of the Cree warriors, whose cultural norm was

Isaac Batt and His Cree Wife

to acquire more than one spouse. Generally speaking, Native men were polygamous and believed that it enhanced a man's standing to have several wives. Samuel Hearne's famous Native guide, Matonabbee, is reputed to have had seven wives, and spoke of their importance: ". . . there is no such thing as travelling any considerable distance or for any length of time, in this country, without *women*."[14] If Batt had more than one wife, he was not the first or only European man to practice polygamy. Many Hudson's Bay Company officers kept more than one Native wife. It was reputed that Moses Norton, while Chief Factor at Prince of Wales Fort at Churchill on Hudson Bay, "kept a harem of a half-dozen of the finest Indian girls."[15]

What is clear and important to our story is that one Native woman, a wife of Isaac Batt, was the mother of Nestichio.

IN HER BIOGRAPHY OF ISAAC BATT, JENNIFER BROWN NOTES that by 1768 he "had established himself as one of the company's more influential servants among the Indians in the vicinity of present day The Pas, Manitoba, and was considered a very honest good Servant."[16]

York Factory's return in furs was diminishing during these years of Batt's service to the Company. In 1773, the return was only eight thousand beaver pelts, a dramatic decrease in the annual average of 30 thousand in the decade before. The reason for this significant drop was the activity of freelance traders, partnerships of independent traders known as "pedlars."

The withdrawal of the French after the Treaty of Paris in 1763 did not prevent this new challenge to the HBC in territory it considered its own. Europe's seemingly insatiable demand for beaver-felt hats fuelled this deep intrusion and intense competition. The pedlars, sometimes called Canadians, had their headquarters in Montreal and were largely funded by Scottish capital. They had a loose organization combining Montreal businessmen, Mixed-blood traders and French Canadian voyageurs. They established a canoe and portage route from Lachine on the St. Lawrence River to Grand Portage on Lake

What Lies Behind the Picture?

Superior and later, further north at Fort William, now Thunder Bay. From there they transported trade goods and supplies to trading posts in the west and brought furs back to Montreal. Like the French independent traders before them, they moved inland and carried on aggressive trading with the Natives. They were consolidated in 1779 as the North West Company (NWC), which was to become the HBC's fiercest rival and by 1800 controlled a majority of the fur trade.

There was opposition within the HBC towards moving inland, but the sustained loss of furs to their competitors demanded a different approach. The decision to move in May 1773 and abandon "its sleep by the frozen sea" was based on recommendations from Andrew Graham, the Chief factor at York Factory, as well as the firsthand experience of men such as Isaac Batt, now recognized as one of the Bay's most experienced inland travellers.[17]

In the spring of 1774, Samuel Hearne and a group of Orkneymen, which probably included the Englishman, Isaac Batt, set out with canoes laden with trading goods and building supplies. They passed numerous favourable trading sites already occupied by the pedlars. On the south shore of Cumberland Lake on "Pine Island" in the Saskatchewan River, Hearne found a desirable spot and established Cumberland House about a hundred kilometres west of the modern day location of The Pas, Manitoba.[18] It was the HBC's first permanent western settlement and eventually proved to be a turning point in the history of the HBC because of its strategic location to an entire system of waterways: westward to the Rockies; north to the Athabasca, and the Peace River Country; east to the Churchill and Nelson Rivers, and Lake Winnipeg and the Red River. The post was about 40 days' paddling time from its supply base at York Factory. The pedlars, however, needed five months to travel from their base in Montreal. To get from Montreal to the Company's inland headquarters on northwestern Lake Superior alone was 2,000 kilometres of rivers, numerous portages and the unpredictable weather of the world's largest lake.

As Batt approached his fifties, he was likely discouraged by

Isaac Batt and His Cree Wife

the Company's failure to promote him. The reason may have been because he was illiterate. He was not unlike numerous other company servants of the mid 1700s.[19] In June 1775, Batt defected and entered the service of the pedlars.

During this period, Batt and his Native wife or wives lived for a year or two upstream from Cumberland House on the south bank of the Saskatchewan River between Nipawin and Fort á La Corne in a house known as "Isaac's House," north of present day Cronlid, Saskatchewan.[20] Thomas Frobisher, an officer with the pedlars, engaged him to serve at this post. As well as being a fur-trading post, it provided provisions for the pedlars whose brigades were journeying eastward to The Grand Portage (after 1803, Fort William) on Lake Superior, and Montreal. Alexander Henry, on his visit to the post, made the following observation: "The quantity of provisions, which I found collected here, exceeded everything of which I had previously formed a notion. In one heap, I saw fifty ton of beef...." Isaac's House was one of the early prairie forts or pemmican posts along the Saskatchewan.[21]

Humphrey Martin, Chief Factor at York, distressed at the loss of a valued employee, sent a personal note urging Batt to return. By the time the letter reached Batt in 1776, he was receptive, "being tired of the Pedlars." He left their employ in the spring of 1777.[22] When George Sutherland, a Company officer, met him on October 13, 1777, Batt was a "freeman," i.e. not indentured to either company, but was soon to return to York Factory and re-engage with the HBC. He may have been in transit at the time, but Sutherland viewed him with suspicion and believed that he was still attached to the French.[23]

When Batt re-entered the HBC's service in 1777, he was described as "a good Moose hunter; but too light to have the command of any place."[24] While lacking in literacy, so important for keeping Company records, Batt excelled as a hunter. The skill of a good moose hunter was recognized as the pinnacle of woodcraft. According to E. T. Seton, the well-known naturalist, "A man may be a good hunter i.e., an all-round trapper and woodman, but not a moose-hunter.... The phrase is not usually qualified;

he is, or is not, a moose-hunter. Just as a man is, or is not, an Oxford M.A."[25]

Although welcomed back, Batt's defection to the pedlars diminished his standing within the HBC. His loyalty was no longer taken for granted, yet inland journals attest to the fact that his usefulness as a hunter, canoe man and trader were still valued well into the 1780s.[26]

By 1791, Isaac Batt was in his sixties. He is described in Company records as, "An old Servant—almost worn out." In May 1791, when Chief Factor Tomison left him at Manchester House—a Bay post on Pine Island which was located on the north bank of the North Saskatchewan River, a few kilometers north east of modern Maidstone, Saskatchewan—he assessed him as "not fitt [sic] for any duty, further than one of the Number [of men there]."[27]

In October of that year, Batt and another trader, John Thompson, went hunting for buffalo, taking six horses, two guns and some supplies. Two Gros Ventre Natives accompanied them.[28] While the accounts of what transpired differ, it would appear that the Natives, "having nothing of their own, were seeking booty. While Batt was handing the Calumet [a pipe, a token of peace and goodwill] to one, the other shot him through the head and together they went off with the whole."[29]

Batt's murder took place on or near Pike's Peak, a day's trek from Manchester House. He was the first Company servant to be killed by Natives in the Saskatchewan District.

When William Tomison learned of Batt's death, he wrote of "the unfortunate end of Isaac Batt, in which he himself [Batt] was highly culpable."[30] While it is only conjecture, it would seem that Batt was considered blameworthy because he had participated in a hunting party that included two Natives known as villains.

Batt adapted successfully to a lifestyle far removed from that which he had known in Hertfordshire, England. His new environment, shared with his Native wife or wives, was to be silent seas of pine, eternal prairies, rushing rivers, and endless winters. His contribution to the Hudson's Bay Company was consider-

Isaac Batt and His Cree Wife

able. Perhaps the most significant example was when he met with the London Committee. Their minutes of May 26, 1773 record the following:

Isaac Batt who returned from that [York] Factory last year having several times attended the Committee, and who had frequently (moved) among the Natives above Basquias [later known as The Pas] 800 miles inland and formerly a settlement or trading house belonging to the French; upon mature deliberation on this matter, it was the opinion of the Committee that it would be for the advantage of the Company trade to establish a settlement inland at or near Basquias. . . .[31]

Isaac Batt, with his considerable inland experience, was likely a major factor in influencing the HBC to move inland from Hudson Bay. This was a strategic move. It enabled the Company to compete with its rivals and to expand its fur trading empire.

It is difficult to escape the conclusion that Isaac Batt, despite his important and long service, was treated poorly by the Company. When he left to go with the pedlars in 1775, the London Committee, perhaps remembering his valuable advice, wrote on August 25, 1777, these words to Henry Marten, the Chief Factor and the Council at York Factory ". . . he never would have deserted your service had it not been for very bad usage."[32]

Our Mixed-blood roots begin with a Native Cree woman. Her name is unknown to us. She was the country wife of English-born Isaac Batt. After his death, our Native ancestor no doubt returned to her family and tribe. Through her daughter, Nestichio, she would pass on her Native heritage to us.

CHAPTER 2

Nestichio Batt and James Spence

OUR STORY CONTINUES THROUGH NESTICHIO, THE DAUGHTER OF ISAAC BATT AND HIS NATIVE WIFE, WHO MARRIES JAMES SPENCE, AN ORCADIAN, WHO LIKE MANY BEFORE HIM LEAVES A WIND-SWEPT ISLAND TO WORK WITH THE HUDSON'S BAY COMPANY IN SNOW-SWEPT RUPERT'S LAND.

WE DO NOT KNOW THE NAME OF ISAAC BATT'S WIDOW, our first Native ancestor, but we do know that of their union, Nestichio Batt was born about 1757. Nestichio married James Spence, an Orcadian[1] who like so many of his countrymen left Orkney to work with the Hudson's Bay Company.

Orkney, a cluster of islands off Scotland's north coast, produced most of the HBC recruits. Orcadians were used to labouring under conditions that were almost as rigorous as those they found in their new land of employment. Many who signed on with the company were likely the sons of crofters or farmers, who were also fishermen. They brought their talents for stonemasonry, coopering, blacksmithing, and boat building to the New World. Their hardiness and adaptability were ideal for manning the distant outposts of the Company.

James Spence was born in 1754 at Howen in the parish of Birsay, the eldest in a family of six. The Reverend George Low, in describing the parish of Birsay in the 1790s, some 20 years after Spence left, noted that it had a population of 1,350, with 144

Nestichio Batt and James Spence

CANADIAN GEOGRAPHIC

resident fishermen constituting the largest occupational group. Low described the men of his parish as " good, honest, manly, decent men ... many 6 feet high; In general, they are very strong men, being hard wrought ... they are, in general, very industrious, and even Laborious...." Low adds that emigration from the parish was common. He writes:

> Numbers of our young people go to sea, to Hudson's Bay, and to trades out of the parish.... None leave the parish for want of employment; indeed, we want hands, because our young fellows go off in hopes of greater wages, as the farmers well feel; the N. W. [North West], etc. being their bate [sic].[2]

Spence, seeking adventure and higher wages, was one of those men who rose to the "bate." He was 19 years old when he signed on in 1773. Like Isaac Batt, he was to become a valued

What Lies Behind the Picture?

employee of the HBC. He began as a labourer and then became a canoe man. He advanced to the position of steersman working inland from York Factory. His superiors described him as "a fine fellow and a good canoe man."[3]

In October 1776, Spence accompanied others on a trade expedition up the North Saskatchewan River. During the trip they passed the Lower (Hudson) House on the North Saskatchewan River where one master[4] and a few men, including Isaac Batt, were residing. This was the first known meeting between Spence and Batt, his future father-in-law.[5] Five years later, Spence married Nestichio Batt, "according to the custom of the country" at or near York Factory. He was 27 and she was 24.

Between 1786 and 1792, Spence worked as a steersman at Cumberland House, Hudson House and Manchester House, the latter about 70 kilometres east of Alberta's current border with Saskatchewan. Steersmen were skilled boatmen. Whether they were guiding a canoe or a York boat, they were responsible for the cargo. Along with the bowmen, they were the best paid and most experienced members of a crew.[6]

Spence and Nestichio wintered on the plains in 1790 in a hunters' encampment made up of two tents housing ten men and a number of wives and children. As well as Spence and his

> The canoes of the fur trade were made of lightweight birch bark. The seams were sewn together with wattappe, roots from the spruce tree made into sinews, and were caulked with the rendered sap or gum of fir, spruce or pine. They ranged in size from 12-metre freighters with a crew of eight to twelve men, carrying their provisions and more than two metric tonnes of cargo, to swifter, smaller vessels, seven to eight metres long. The smaller craft were used for more rapid transport because they were more manageable for the often numerous and lengthy portages. They had a carrying capacity of one-and-a-half tonnes and could be paddled by four to six men and portaged by two.

Running the rapids on Mattawa River
FRANCIS ANNE HOPKINS, NATIONAL ARCHIVES OF CANADA

family, there were William Flett and James Batt (Isaac Batt's brother and Nestichio's uncle). All were skilled hunters who kept the HBC well supplied with fresh meat.[7]

During the 1780s the inland posts were few but by the 1790s the HBC was rapidly expanding its fur trading posts throughout the Nelson River and Athabasca Districts in order to keep pace with its rival, the North West Company.

The HBC needed men who were experienced enough to be sent inland. They had to know the water systems and the languages of the Native people, and they had to win the trust of the indigenous hunters. James, with the assistance of Nestichio, would fit these qualifications. Unlike Isaac Batt, Spence had something

> As a child, Spence, like other Orcadians, had the benefit of a school system far superior to that of England. In 1696 Scotland's Parliament passed its "Act for Setting Schools." A school was established in every parish in Scotland and Orkney that did not already have one so both girls and boys could learn to read Holy Scripture. It was not until the 1880s that England caught up to her northern neighbours in literacy.[8]

What Lies Behind the Picture?

that was invaluable to the HBC. He was literate and therefore could keep the records which were so important in running a post.

James Spence and Nestichio were settled at a fort, which in this period was more like a small shanty. It was located at Split Lake on the Nelson River about 300 kilometres southwest of York Factory. Spence's letter of March 17, 1791, to Joseph Colen at York Factory gives us an intimate look at life as he experienced it:

Honoured Sir,

I received your letter of 12th January and am sorry to hear of your great disappointment of my not letting you know what Indians have visited me, or what furs they brought, there were very few of them. Na-nas-hanow and his Gang [Band] *arrived here in the fall and has remained near us all winter, what furs and provisions they had to spare they traded with me. Wappetunish, I-as-su-es-cum, Pe-pu-new-hum and Kish-e-howm-skin with all their followers have brought a few skins throughout the winter when they wanted a drink of Brandy. I do not think they have been with the Canadians* [North West Company] *as yet. Tho* [sic] *they are hunting between us and them. Assisish and his followers have traded a few skins and provisions . . . I have given James Batt and John Allen a supply of tobacco and ammunition and sent them out with Indians to keep them from visiting the Canadian Traders and to encourage all Indians to go down to York* [Factory] *and likewise given to Jemmy Jock an Indian who assisted us tobacco and ammunition and sent him after Messegommowithow and the other Indians . . . (whom I have not seen since they left us.) Likewise to go after the Musqua Rat River Indians. I told him to cut tobacco to all Leaders he fell in with to encourage them to go down with their furs in the summer to the* [York] *Factory. It was late in the season before we got up here* [so] *that very few of the Indians knew of Englishmen* [likely Orcadian traders] *being in the quarter as yet, but I think many furs may have been traded from Indians with Plenty of Goods and proper men to conduct canoes for Indians cannot steer over*[ly] *large ones.*

Nestichio Batt and James Spence

> *The Canadian Settlement* [NWC] *is five days journey distance from us, they have each two canoes and 10 or 12 men as I am informed by the Natives. They have been sending men with rum and goods to wherever Natives are tenting to get their furs from them and are very liberal in distributing their rum to Indians.*
>
> *Cloth is the chief article called for by Natives and Brandy you know they all love, as for other articles of trading goods it is called for as they stand in need of it. We have been and are now much in want of provisions, which is the reason of my send[ing] two men down with the Indians. I can do very well without them and they may be useful at the factory. You will be so good to let me know how I shall do with the articles that will remain. I expect the tobacco will not be expended this spring the Indians say it is very bad I can put it in a keg and lay it in the ground as for the guns, I have no Indians that will trade, the locks are so bad; these I cannot lay up you will be so good as to send word how I shall do.*[9]

Spence goes on to write that in order to survive he has to pay a considerable amount for provisions from the few Natives who remain in the area. The rest had left because their source of food, the moose, was so scarce. He continues:

> *This is the poorest year that I have ever had, and the men are continually chiding me about their poor living. I wish from my heart that I had not undertaken the charge, but I did it unthinkingly without considering what a heavy burden I was loading on myself, as it is, we have great reason to be thankful to God Almighty that it has not been worse when I consider that all the Indians left us in the manner they did and they all thought we had returned to the factory. However I have done all that lies in my power for the Interest of the Honorable Company and likewise to gain the favour of the Indians. I have only 500 Beaver as yet in furs, but as I have some brandy left expect to trade some more.*
>
> *I Remain*
> *Your very dutiful servant*
> *James Spence.*[10]

What Lies Behind the Picture?

In this bird's-eye view into the life and times of a fur trader, we see the efforts and frustrations of a Company employee seeking to gain and maintain trade with the Natives. It is significant that in his association with the Native people he knows many well enough to call them by name. Likely Nestichio was able to assist him both in communicating and maintaining a level of trust with the Natives. These qualities and skills were passed on to her by her Native mother and were vital in assisting Spence in his function as a fur trader. He had to compete with an ever-present rival, the North West Company, who like himself as a Bay servant was not above using brandy or rum as an acceptable means to obtain furs.

We can also get a glimpse of the post's dependence on the Native community, not only for trade, but also for provisions and information about its competitors. We can gather from the correspondence that Spence was a literate, religious and a loyal Company servant who is apologetic for not doing well with the small quantity of goods put in his care. The letter reveals the severe emotional and physical strain on him which possibly contributed to his early death.

JAMES SPENCE AND NESTICHIO WERE SETTLED, DURING THE summer of 1792, at Buckingham House, on the north bank of the North Saskatchewan not far from present day Elk Point, Alberta.[11] The fort had been established to compete with the North West Company's Fort George, which was just a musket shot away. The posts were a short distance from one another in order to join forces if there was a Native attack. Instrumental in setting up the HBC fort was the Chief Factor, and Orcadian, William Tomison.[12]

Buckingham House had a population of 37 men, all of them Orkneymen except the English surveyor, Peter Fidler, an American, and two (French) Canadians. Likely, a number of these men had Native wives and family. The predominance of Orcadians at Buckingham House was typical of inland posts of the day.

Nestichio Batt and James Spence

Though quartered at Buckingham House, Spence and Nestichio and their family appear to have spent the winters in hunting camps providing meat and furs for the post.

In 1794, Spence was asked to be summer "Master" at Buckingham House. Nestichio, his wife, and their four children lived with him in the married quarters. Their accommodation would be minimal: one room furnished with bunk beds, table and chairs and a fireplace for cooking and warmth. Spence remained in charge of Buckingham House for the next 18 months while Tomison was away, possibly establishing Edmonton House. A year before, Tomison had sent Peter Fidler, William Flett and two others to seek out a possible site for Edmonton House, which was eventually built in 1795.

Early records indicate that Nestichio was a remarkable woman. As it was common for children of mixed-blood to be raised among their mother's people, they frequently became indistinguishable from the Native people, as Nestichio's name would testify.[13] According to one translation, Nestichio in Cree is *Nestichiowick,* meaning three persons in one, that is, having three guardian spirits.[14]

One of the skills Nestichio would have learned from her Native mother was the art of trapping or snaring small fur-bearing animals, such as marten, weasel, rabbit and muskrat. She would have also learned practical things about skinning animals, softening leather, sewing moccasins, stringing snowshoes, gutting fish and making fire out of a fire bag. Like the other women, she would be of great assistance in provisioning the post not only with furs but also with fish and partridge.[15]

The journal of Thomas Staynor, Chief Factor at York Factory during the 1790s, describes a frightening episode involving Nestichio. While at Manchester House, she and another woman and their children had gone to the plains to bring in meat from a felled buffalo cow. Staynor writes:

> *While they were engaged in cutting up the carcass they were attacked by a gray wolf,* [which was likely rabid] *and which had already devoured a dog belonging to the party. One of the women, possibly Nestichio, warded off the wolf with a*

What Lies Behind the Picture?

knife and a hatchet before retreating to the safety of the encampment with the children.[16]

In late October of 1795, Spence fell ill. Tomison, upon hearing of his illness, wrote to him:

I was sorry to find you enjoyed so ill a state of health as to despair of recovery, but God's will be done, and may we all be enabled by His holy word to prepare for that change which must come sooner or later. . . . So conclude wishing you a better state of health, and success to the Company's affairs I remain your humble servant, Willm. Tomison. P.S. Please to return my most grateful thanks to Mr. Shaw [of NWC] for his attention to you.[17]

On November 27, 1795, James Spence died at the age of 42 years. His wages were duly listed as £25 per annum, and his employment as that of a "steersman." His salary of £6 in 1774–75 had risen to £25. The post journal records: "About midnight James Spence departed this life, having made his will to his wife and four children." The following day a joiner from the North West's Fort George constructed a coffin. On Sunday afternoon James Spence was "entered [sic] . . . with all the formalities due."[18] Recent discoveries have established his final resting place. His remains are buried within the palisades of what was Buckingham House. His legacy was left to his wife Nestichio, daughter of the deceased Isaac Batt, and their four children.[19] Five years after his death the HBC committee wrote to the Chief Factor of York Factory:

The late Mr. James Spence Senr bequeathed £375 Three per Cent Consolidated Bank Annuities between his Children in Hudson Bay. You are therefore desired to send home Annually a Certificate of their being living that [the] Amount of the Dividend in Goods may be Yearly delivered to them by you as is done with other Children under like Circumstances.[20]

As if the tardiness of the HBC in honouring the legacy was not enough, the estate of James Spence was claimed by his father, Nicol Spence, thus preventing it from going to James' family. This is all the more startling as the father likely resided in

Nestichio Batt and James Spence

Orkney. What was his motivation? Greed? Racism? It is possible that he believed the country marriage of his son and Nestichio was not a legal marriage and that the offspring of the marriage were not legitimate and therefore Nestichio and the children were not entitled to share James' estate when he died. William Tomison, out of kindness and respect for Spence and Nestichio, took on the responsibility for the care of Nestichio and the four children.

According to HBC documents from 1806, the father relinquished his claim only to the *interest* that had accumulated. This allowed "the Executor to pay occasionally £20 to the Company for the use of his (Spence's) children's upkeep but (it goes on to state) we understand, they have been supplied frequently with goods, by Wm. Tomison." To make sure that the family did not go over what they owed the company store, the document adds, "we desire you will let us know the whole amount of the Goods, which they have from time to time, been supplied with since their father's death, and should they have been overpaid that we may recover back the Surplus from the Executor."[21]

There is very little information on the lives of Nestichio and their children following James' death. We do know that Nestichio was never to have the full benefit of her husband's legacy.

James Jr. and Andrew were still living at Buckingham House in 1796–97, and were old enough to accompany the men on trips as far as Edmonton House or to the "hunters' tent."[22] With the closure of Buckingham House, we lose track of Nestichio and the family until their appearance, many years later, in the Red River Settlement, which had become a retirement community for many fur-trade families from across the western plains.

The Settlement was along the banks of the Red and Assiniboine Rivers. Where the two rivers joined was called The Forks and marked the location of HBC's Fort Garry. The area is now part of the city of Winnipeg, Manitoba. The Settlement was founded in 1811 by a Scot, Lord Selkirk (Thomas Douglas) 5th Earl of Selkirk. He was a major owner of the HBC and obtained from the company a grant of 300,000 square kilometers in the Red and Assiniboine river valleys. Following the

What Lies Behind the Picture?

Highland Clearances, when thousands of tenants were dispossessed of their land by their "lairds" in favour of sheep farms, Selkirk sought to relocate many in Rupert's Land in what became the Red River Settlement. The first party reached its destination in 1812 and subsequent groups arrived in 1813 and 1814 when a fortified house called Fort Douglas was built on the west side of the Red River opposite the NWC's Fort Gibralter. As more settlers arrived the NWC saw them as a direct threat to its trading interests and so it harassed and then drove the colonists away. The HBC restored the settlement but it was dispersed once again by the Nor'Westers after the Seven Oaks Massacre.[23] In 1817 Lord Selkirk arrived with a military force of mercenaries and reestablished the colony. In the process he brought the NWC trade to a standstill by occupying Fort William, its principal depot. He bought £100,000 worth of its furs, which he eventually returned, but the NWC missed a year of revenue and their trade was completely disrupted.[24] Selkirk's intervention insured that the Red River colony survived.

Likely after the colony had returned to stability, Nestichio and her family joined the growing number of Company families and freemen, who were encouraged by the HBC to take up residence in the settlement. Nestichio died December 3, 1827, at the age of 70 and is buried at St. John's Anglican Church at Red River.[25]

In May 1834, the Spence children petitioned the HBC for a final disposition of their father's remaining estate. James Jr. acted as executor and requested that the estate, which amounted to £334, be divided into four equal portions. James Jr. was apparently illiterate. Two witnesses verified his mark on the petition. A note appended to the petition said, "as the parties are much in want, I would strongly recommend, Your honoring the money to be placed at once to their respective credits."[26] We do not know the final outcome of this request.

James Spence Sr. and Nestichio had four children: James, Andrew, George, and Margaret. The eldest, James Spence Jr. carries the story forward. He married Mary, a Stone[27] (Assiniboine).

Nestichio Batt and James Spence

Barbara Spence, our great-great grandmother was born from this union. She married Thomas Wishart, our great-great grandfather, and we will return to their story later.

WILLIAM AND SASKATCHEWAN

CHAPTER 3

A Country Marriage

WE LEAVE THE BATT/SPENCE STORY TO INTRODUCE ANOTHER LINE OF OUR ANCESTRY. THIS LINE BEGINS WITH ANOTHER ORCADIAN, WILLIAM FLETT, WHO, AIDED BY HIS COUNTRY WIFE, SASKATCHEWAN, BECOMES A VALUED HUNTER AND BOATMAN ADVANCING TO THE POSITION OF MASTER AT SEVERAL HUDSON'S BAY COMPANY POSTS INCLUDING FORT EDMONTON.

WILLIAM A. FLETT WAS BORN AROUND 1762 IN THE Redland district of the parish of Firth, in Orkney.[1] He signed on with the Hudson's Bay Company on June 19, 1782, at the age of 20, some 20 years after James Spence Sr.

Flett arrived on August 15, 1782 by ship at York Factory, which was under the command of Humphrey Martin.[2] Barely had he settled in as a labourer when the post was attacked on August 24 by a French force comprised of three ships and 290 soldiers, under the command of Compte de Laperouse. On Sunday September 1, 1782, the York Factory journal entry reads, "This day the Factory was burnt & all the remaining of the Company's Servants & the French Troops embarked in the Seven Sloops for the French Fleet."[3] The attackers left York Factory, in the words of William Tomison, "a Ruinous heap, which is a Disagreeable sight to behold."[4]

Flett was among those taken prisoner. He was imprisoned in France before returning in 1783 to help reconstruct York Factory, which had by then been reclaimed from the French.

A Country Marriage

York boat crew
PROVINCIAL ARCHIVES OF ALBERTA B.5857

The HBC was desperate for good men. It needed hard-working employees who were prepared to endure hunger and hardship, merciless cold and insect-ridden heat.[5] The Company found no equal to the sturdy, thrifty and usually sober Orkney men.[6] They undoubtedly welcomed Flett's return to honour his contract.

Following his return, he was employed as a labourer, steersman and hunter, both inland and at York Factory, from 1783 to 1809. In 1790, he was in a winter camp with James Spence Sr. and Nestichio and her uncle, James Batt. The men were spoken of as skilled hunters.[7] Flett was 28 years old.

In 1793, Flett rode on horseback in company with Peter Fidler, the English surveyor, in search of a new site for a Hudson's Bay Company post, a post that would become known as Edmonton House. It was the beginning of April and spring was in the air. Ice and snow no longer had a grip on the land. Thickets of aspen had not yet flowered but Red Osier dogwood flaunted its colour against the modest green of

What Lies Behind the Picture?

spruce and jack pine. Beaked Hazelnut with tiny flame flowers caught Fidler's eye.

Fidler wrote in his Journal in 1793:

The Canadians [North West Company], *speak of going higher up the Saskatchewan River to build—induced by Tomison* [Chief Factor at Buckingham House] *to send me up there, to see where would be the most eligible spot to build at should the Canadians go there—Mr.Thomas Thomas Junr. Surgeon, John Ward & William Flett accompanied me.*[8]

On their way John Ward got lost but was able to find his way back to Buckingham House. Fidler, Flett and Thomas continued the journey. They travelled about 200 kilometres along the north bank of the North Saskatchewan River for seven days until they came to the mouth of the Sturgeon River some 3 kilometres opposite present day Fort Saskatchewan where they scouted possible sites for a post.[9]

On April 7th, Fidler wrote:

At 8:15 a.m. we reasumed [sic] *our Journey—went SbW* [South by West] *3 miles thro some small hammocks of asp & willow & came to the edge of a pretty large plain with good decent* [sic] *all the way down to the river—here we got sight of the Rocky Mountains which appeared very plane like towering black clouds in a summer evening when calm. This view was obtained a little way from the Wood edge in the Plain—2 or 3 small ponds of water near—crossed over the Plain WbW* [West by West] *5 miles—then thro several small hammocks of small asp SWbW* [South West by West] *& arrived upon the bank of the Tea River or Red Willow creek sometimes called the Sturgeon River at 11 AM. It is about twenty yards wide, strong current & pretty deep.... This sturgeon or Tea river is at the end of journey but not a proper place to build at owing to the small woods that are here ... in the Year 1795 Edmonton House was built which is about 1 mile higher up the Saskatchewan river than the mouth of this river ... no wood to build with there but what was rafted down the river."*

A Country Marriage

Fidler goes on to write:

The above observation taken at the confluence of the Tea [Sturgeon] and Saskatchewan Rivers—In crossing this last plain my Compass fell down & unluckly [sic] broke—but I had got near my Journey, and at 3 PM we returned back for Buckingham House on the same side of the river—& nearly the same track we came—put up at 5 PM—after going about 6 miles—Wm Flett killed 1 red deer."[10]

In addition to a detailed travelogue and a description of the terrain travelled by the party, Fidler kept a short table of the distances and the times he was at various locations.

The sod turning for Edmonton House took place on October 3, 1795, at a site about two kilometres from the area explored by Fidler, Flett and Thomas in 1793 west of present day Fort Saskatchewan. According to Fidler, it took 28 minutes to walk from the "Tea river or red willow creek" to the fort.[11] The actual construction of Edmonton House began October 13, 1795,[12] and as Fidler observed, all the wood had to be rafted down by water there being no wood near where the fort was erected. Poling rafts of logs was not only strenuous but hazardous work. Trimming and setting the posts into the ground for the palisades while the temperature kept dropping added to the men's discomfort. With great relief the post's flag was raised on December 7, just upstream from the mouth of the Sturgeon and just opposite, or "a musket shot" away from Fort Augustus, which had been erected by the North West Company in the summer of 1795.[13] The two forts stood in splendid isolation vying with each other for an advantage in a lucrative trading location. Duncan McGillivray, a young clerk employed by the North West Company, described the area as being "a rich and plentiful country abounding with all kinds of animals, especially Beaver and Otters, which are said to be so numerous that the Women and Children kill them with sticks and hatchets."[14] There were frequent feuds between the two companies. They had built close to one another, however, in order to join forces because of the ever-present danger of raids by the Gros Ventre and Blackfoot.[15]

What Lies Behind the Picture?

Hudson's Bay Company crest, Lower Fort Garry
VERNON R. WISHART

WHAT WERE THE CIRCUMSTANCES THAT BROUGHT TOGETHER a man from barren Orkney and a Cree woman raised in the woodlands and plains of Rupert's Land? According to Governor George Simpson's journal, Saskatchewan was closely associated with Fort Carlton.[16] Her name is derived from the Cree word *kis-is-ska,* meaning "rapid" and *tche-wan,* meaning "current;" hence, the river with the rapid current, *kis-is-ska-tche-wan sipiy.*[17] (*Sipiy* is the Cree word for river.) The traders likely transposed the Cree to Saskatchewan, which became the name of a province and two rivers, the North and South Saskatchewan. She would have spoken of herself as Kis-is-ska-tche-wan.

One can imagine that Flett first noticed her among the cluster of teepees that were located outside Fort Carlton where he

A Country Marriage

stopped on journeys to and from York Factory. Probably she was among the Home Guard Indians, who lived close to the post and were employed by the Company as hunters and guides.

By the time Flett joined the HBC, marriage with Native women had become a normal part of fur trade social life. Though entries about Native women are sparse and fragmented, their union with traders is reflected in the journals and archival records of the early to late 1800s. The acceptance of these unions is reflected in the widespread use of the descriptive phrase—marriage "according to the custom of the country" or "à la façon du pays."[18] The Cree word for such marriages was *wikihtowin* and the couple as *nápem and wikimakan*—husband and wife.

The Hudson's Bay Company Committee in London discouraged, at least initially, liaisons between its employees and Native women. Its bitter rival, the North West Company, inherited the pattern adopted by the early French traders and encouraged country relationships for its own benefit. The HBC gradually saw the wisdom of this. When William Flett began his service in 1782, it was not uncommon for HBC men to marry Native women according to the custom of the country.

With the completion of his second term, Flett likely took more than a passing interest in Saskatchewan. At age 28, he was still unmarried. She was in her teens, and by Native standards of the time, of marriageable age. We do not know the personal details but can imagine that he noticed her among the Home Guard going about her tasks; the great care she took in fashioning her hair in knots and plait; the adorning of her buckskin garments with beads. Perhaps he had managed to meet her as she made her way from the river to the fort. Did her gaze meet his? Did they brush in passing? Was there an unspoken bond that began to develop between them? Did their attraction grow as she accompanied the canoes on their inland voyages or the men on hunting excursions? Or did she have a choice? We can only guess at intimacy, and never know the story.

On inland journeys Native men and woman accompanied Company men. The men acted as guides, hunted for game and

What Lies Behind the Picture?

acted as interpreters in the Native tongue. The women did the cooking, assisted in carrying supplies on portages, repaired equipment, made moccasins and performed all the necessary maintenance tasks required for going forth to trade and returning with boats laden with fur. Sylvia Van Kirk writes that women were so important that "inland trips which were not accompanied by Indian women seemed doomed to failure."[19]

On these trips inland, Flett and Saskatchewan were possibly drawn closer together and their affection for one another nurtured as they shared in the strenuous daily routine.

When he was not engaged with the boat brigades going to and fro from York Factory, Flett's duty was to hunt and supply meat for the fort. Records show that in the winter of 1796–97, he hunted buffalo.[20] Native women skinned the fallen animals and prepared the hides and the meat for transport by dog sled in winter and travois in summer.

Flett and Saskatchewan may have found themselves in the same hunting parties. Did she watch anxiously during the summer hunts when he rode into a buffalo herd at great speed, aiming, firing, reloading while guiding the horse with his knees? It meant certain death or injury to fall off a running horse amidst stampeding buffalo. Did she run past markers thrown beside fallen buffalo by the Native hunters to mark their kill, to those thrown down by Flett?[21]

Saskatchewan was 15 or 16 when Flett, approaching 30, asked her father if they might be married in a manner acceptable to the Cree standards.[22] The Cree considered it an honour to have one of their women selected as the wife of a trader. Flett knew that most native families were not upset when a daughter married a trader. It brought certain advantages, such as status and material benefits. Would Saskatchewan's father be pleased at this request or would he be wary? Other Native women had been abandoned by husbands returning to their homeland.

In her father's eyes this daughter may have been special, for she had been named after the North Saskatchewan River around which so much of their life centered. Was this man named Flett a suitable partner for his daughter? Flett had qualities that must

A Country Marriage

Woman with child—wife of John Rowand Jr.
CITY OF EDMONTON ARCHIVES, EA-10-1651

have made him seem a suitable husband. He was mature, strong and an expert canoe man. He had become skilled in hunting, so much so that he was often called upon to go with Native hunters to kill game for food for the fort. More important, he met Natives on an equal footing and seemed to enjoy their company. Though he was not Cree, he blended easily into their surroundings.

What Lies Behind the Picture?

Buffalo chase: to Red River and beyond
GLENBOW ARCHIVES

Killing a buffalo was no easy task. The largest land mammal on the North American continent, a bull, could weigh up to 900 kilograms and was dangerous when wounded. The name buffalo originated with early French explorers who called them Boeufs, meaning oxen. The name went through several changes ranging from *buffle* to *buffalo* and finally to *buffalo*. Scientists prefer *bison* but both names are now used. Natives traditionally have had a deep spiritual connection to the buffalo, for the animal meant sustenance and survival.

A Country Marriage

William Flett would follow the practice of the times in his marriage to Saskatchewan. He would ask her father, and under certain conditions the union would be arranged. He promised to give the father some blankets, a few shirts, a musket, powder and shot, tobacco and tools, after which they arrived at a mutual agreement.[23]

The marriage likely took place in the Cree encampment. It did not involve exchanging of vows but was solemnized by words from the elders and other rituals such as the smoking and the passing of the calumet, a long stemmed ceremonial pipe, as a token of peace and goodwill. Flett would be expected to visit the father's tent to claim his wife. He and Saskatchewan would then be ceremoniously escorted to the fort.[24]

Sylvia Van Kirk adds this observation: "At the North West Company posts, wives were clothed in 'Canadian fashion' which consisted of shirt, short gown, petticoat and leggings. Then the trader conducted his bride to his quarters, and from thenceforth they were considered to be man and wife."[25] There are no records indicating the practice of the Hudson's Bay Company traders, but it can be assumed that they followed this same ritual.[26] The marriage also included the expectation that Flett would spend time with Saskatchewan's family.

B<small>Y THE TIME OF THEIR MARRIAGE, F</small>LETT <small>HAD ALREADY</small> learned skills that were seasonally useful. Saskatchewan's country skills helped further his advancement from a labourer and canoe man to that of steersman, the man responsible for the safe delivery of the Company's goods. This was no easy task, given the treacherous waterways and rapids that often faced the boatmen. A veteran of the brigades, Flett would be expected to keep the party on pace as their fur-laden boats made their way to York Factory on the shores of Hudson Bay as well as their return laden with trade goods and supplies for the isolated forts in Rupert's Land.

In the spring, the annual boat brigades loaded with fur

What Lies Behind the Picture?

commenced their journey down the main river-ways to York Factory. It is difficult to imagine the strenuous life these trips entailed. The party arose very early in the morning and paddled several hours until 8:00 A.M. After an hour's paddling, the boatmen took breaks for a smoke. A voyage was measured in pipes. As speed was important, they carried food with them. Lunch at noon consisted of a piece of pemmican, often eaten while still paddling. The voyage continued until 9:00 P.M. when they stopped to make camp. Evening meals consisted largely of *rouchou* or pemmican soup and strong tea. Before bedding down for a few hours of sleep, the men often entertained themselves with songs and stories.

When the men came to rapids, waterfalls or stretches of low water, they portaged, emptying the boats and carrying them and their cargo around the obstacles. Four men carried the canoes upside down on their shoulders. With the advent of the York boats, 'tracking' was required. Teams of men working from the banks of the river dragged the boats by ropes while Flett as steersman guided the boat's course. It was exhausting work. When it was necessary to bring the boats ashore to portage around falls or rapids, the men carried or shoved or pulled them by ropes over round logs to propel them forward. They packed the cargo of supplies, furs and trade goods in 40-kilogram bundles and carried them in a sling that went around the man's forehead and swung down his back. While carrying these massive loads—some men carried two bundles—the voyageurs, amidst shouts of encouragement from Flett, had to climb rocky banks, skirt marshy areas and penetrate dense bush. After the portage, it was not unusual for them to be up to their waists in icy waters as they reloaded the boats. At night Flett and his party would often roll themselves up in their blankets, dead tired.

A few years after his marriage to Saskatchewan, Flett was appointed "Master". The Master held a respected position in the Company. His job was to be in charge of outposts, which he and the men under him had set up to trade with Native bands. Flett's work in various capacities along the North Saskatchewan, his

A Country Marriage

At the portage: HBC employees on their annual expedition
H.A. OGDEN, NATIONAL ARCHIVES OF CANADA

The York boats replaced the canoe as the most common means of transporting furs and goods.[27] They could carry nearly five metric tonnes, twice the load of a large canoe but with the same number of men. They were modelled after the Orkney fishing boats or yawls, which dated back to Viking influences. Made of wood with tamarak for the keel, they were 12 metres in length. An eight-man crew propelled the boats with oars, ropes and, when the wind was right, a sail.

What Lies Behind the Picture?

knowledge of Cree and of Native ways through Saskatchewan; and his ability to read and write adequately, in order to keep company records, gave him the necessary background for the task.[28]

William Flett's appointments as Master signalled not only the trust the HBC had in him, but also the level of regard with which he and Saskatchewan were held by Native people.

By 1813, Flett had developed his skills in constructing canoes to such an extent that he was designated as "Master and Canoe Builder" or "Master and Canoe man." No doubt Saskatchewan continued to play an important role. She likely helped women at the post to collect *wattappe,* the roots from the spruce tree. These roots were made into sinewy thread, which the women used to sew the seams of the canoes. Large quantities of *wattappe* were needed, as was spruce gum which was used for caulking.[29]

In their shared skills, Flett and Saskatchewan served the HBC at several posts over the years, including several years at Edmonton House (Fort Edmonton). It would be largely in the environs of Edmonton House that they would raise their four children, Elizabeth born in 1799; Anne (Nancy) born in 1800; followed by William Jr. born in 1809, and Peter born in 1811.

CHAPTER 4

Flett's Journal at Edmonton House

IN WHICH FLETT IS LEFT IN CHARGE OF EDMONTON HOUSE [FORT EDMONTON] WHERE HIS JOURNAL ENTRIES GIVE US A GLIMPSE INTO THE DAILY ROUTINE AND THE DECISIONS NECESSARY TO MAINTAIN ONE OF THE BUSIEST OF HBC TRADING POSTS; AND SADLY, DURING THE SAME PERIOD THE EMERGENCE OF RACISM WITHIN THE RED RIVER SETTLEMENT AND THE RANKS OF THE HBC.

IN MAY 1819, WILLIAM FLETT TOOK CHARGE OF EDMONTON House. The occasion was the departure of Francis Heron, the Chief Trader, with the annual fur-bearing boat brigades for York Factory.

The departure of the brigades was marked by the excitement of the crowds on the river-bank, and the boatmen's anticipation of what lay ahead. When the boats were loaded and ready, they swung out into the main current at a signal from Heron, following one behind the other in a long single file. Men waved their hats and paddles to their wives and children, as well as to the Company servants and Natives gathered on the shore. As the swift current of the North Saskatchewan River carried the boats around the first bend in the river, someone would start a boat song and the others would join in. Their laughter and song downstream were in sharp contrast to the back-breaking labour, sweat and swearing that would mark the portages and towing of cumbersome cargo when they returned upstream in September. What a sight for tired bodies as the cannon fired, and people from the fort and teepees lined the banks to welcome them back.

What Lies Behind the Picture?

While Heron's brigade disappeared into the distance, to be joined by other boats at Fort Pitt and again at Fort Carlton, William Flett settled into his task of supervising the work at Edmonton House.

In the *Journal of Occurrences at Edmonton House—May 17, 1819 to September 23, 1819*, Flett makes daily entries a sample of which follow:[1]

May 1819

Tuesd 18th On Mr. Heron's departure yesterday with his Boats and Canoes for York Factory he left me in charge of this District for the summer [Likely Edmonton and the surrounding area. Possibly Saskatchewan District which stretched north to Lesser Slave Lake, south to the U.S. border, west to the Rockies and east to Fort Carlton]... *At 10 AM James Spence, Peter Flett and Mr. Hugh Munroe returned from Beaver River to which place they were sent some time ago by Mr. Heron with Pemmican for the Northern Departments. The people employed planting potatoes in the gardens—Mild Weather Wind S.W.*

Thursd 20th People employed as yesterday [The wives, Native, Metis and Mixed-blood, were responsible for the making of pemmican, the maintenance of the gardens and the bringing in of the crops]. *Sewed some turnip seeds and planted the last of our potatoes of which we have planted in all about 24 Bushels. Sewed also about 6 Bushels of Barley & 2 Bushels of Wheat...*

Thursd 27th John Ward arrived from the Horse tent at 4 PM [The horses were likely kept near Lac la Nonne, 60 kilometres northeast of Edmonton House and/or Hairy Hill, 80 kilometres east] *He informed me that several of our Horses have been killed by the Wolves They are unusually numerous at this place Cold Cloudy Weather Wind N.W...*

June 1819

Tuesd 1st The people employed squaring and hauling Logs for House Building The Boat builders and Blacksmith employed at their respective trades Windy Weather W

Thursd 3rd... at 7 A.M sent Mr. Munro and one of Mr.

Flett's Journal at Edmonton House

William Flett
SHIRLEY WISHART

Houses [?] little Boys to look for some horses that strayed away some time ago. At 2 P.M. Mr. Munro returned to acquaint me that in searching through the Woods for the Horses he and his companion parted from each other and notwithstanding he made every search for the Boy. He could not fall in with him—I immediately sent off two men for the Boy and hope they will succeed in finding him—Rained at intervals all day Winds—N.W

What Lies Behind the Picture?

Frid 4th At 11 A.M the men whom I sent in search of Mr Houses Boy returned but did not succeed in finding him.

Frid 11th About 10 A.M the men sent off in search of Mr Houses Boy on the 3rd Instant returned but after all their endeavors did not succeed in finding him although they fell in with his track several times

Sund 13th About 3 P.M. one of our Hunters came to the House to acquaint me that he and his tent mate had the carcasses of two moose and a Stag at their Tents—Rained all day froze a little towards night W S.W. . . .

July 1819

Frid 2nd About 11 A.M sent off James Whiteway [?], Peter Flett and Donald Johnstone in Company with people from the N.W House [North West Company] *to reestablish Acton House in conformity with the orders I received from Mr Heron to that effect on his departure from here in the Spring. Acton House is situated on this River about 50 miles.*

Saturd 24th The people commenced cutting Hay. Our crop of Barley Wheat & Potatoes have a beautiful appearance

Wednesd 28th About 9 PM 3 Beaver [Hill] *Cree Indians arrived from Carlton District with the intent we suppose of thieving our Horses*

August 1819

Mond 2nd All the men at work and the women at the Fort employed making Hay

Tuesd 3rd About 3 PM the Beaver Hill Cree went off for their own country but I am apprehensive they intend to make a search for our horses as it is not likely they would come so great a distance for the purpose of horse thieving and return without effecting their purpose

Frid 6th Early this morning George Ward, Joseph Bouchien and an Indian, who went with the Horses to Red [Deer] *River last spring returned after having affected in taking the Horses there safe. Although they had many Narrow Escapes among the Stone Indians. At 1PM two Blood Indians arrived for tobacco for a band of that tribe who are to arrive tomorrow to trade.*

Flett's Journal at Edmonton House

September 1819

Frid 10th People employed reaping Barley of which we shall have a very fine crop

Thursd 16th People employed getting wood for boat building

Sund 19th Last night the Beaver Cree Indians stole Four Horses from the N.W. [North West Company] *House*

Thursd 23rd About 6 PM Mr Hughes and the N.W. partner arrived from Fort William accompanied by two of his clerks by whom I am informed that they left their Canoes within 3 days march of this place

At 11 PM Mr Heron arrived from York Factory accompanied by Mr James Bird Junior [probably Jamie Bird, the son of James Bird, the Chief Factor]. *Mr Heron left three of his Boats a short distance above Cumberland with the fourth kept company with the N.W.* [North West Company] *canoes for the purpose of* [transporting] *a supply of goods to Acton House in company with our opponents.*

I now of course resign the charge of this place to Mr Heron by whom this journal will be continued.

Signed by Wm Flett Senr [Flett's personal signature]

Flett's entries give us an insight into life at the fort from spring through to fall. The routine of maintaining the fort is also marked by what appears to be the tragic loss of a boy despite search parties sent on June 3rd and June 4th. Anxious eyes must have awaited his return, hoping he would find his way home. When he didn't another search party was sent out on June 11th, perhaps at the parents' urging. There is no entry marking his return.

Edmonton House was, even at this date, a hub for the fur trade, a supplier of horses and a boat-building center. From the fort's journal we can establish that the production of the famous York boats was an important activity. Governor George Simpson, after the union of the two companies in 1821, was to accelerate the construction of these sturdy boats.

The costly enmity between the HBC and the NWC was making the rivals realize that they must join forces. One early signal was Mr. Heron's arrival at Edmonton House with the North West men and

What Lies Behind the Picture?

their canoes; together they would supply goods to Acton House near present-day Rocky Mountain House, where both companies had established posts in 1799. Flett, nevertheless, still makes note of the NWC in his last entry on Sept. 23rd as "our opponents."

On January 4, 1819, Heron writes, "During my absence leaving William Flette [often spelt with a final e] in charge;" indicating that Flett was frequently put in charge while senior officers were travelling. The HBC archives also record him as Master at Acton House during 1810–12,[2] and Master, Canoe man at Rocky Mountain House in 1821[3] before becoming Master, Canoe man at Edmonton House. In the record of Edmonton District Accounts 1821–22, William A. Flette is recorded as 55 in age, from the Parish of Firth (Orkney). He is listed as 2nd Trader having 38 years of service and receiving £40 in wages. It appears that his contract with the HBC ended in 1822.[4]

Flett and Saskatchewan retired to the Red River settlement in 1823. He died shortly afterwards, on November 10, 1823. He was buried by the Anglican missionary David Jones in the churchyard of St. John's Cathedral, the cemetery of the Hudson's Bay Company.[5] As he approached death, he made his will, which was a testimonial of the love and esteem he held for Saskatchewan. He directed that all his monies be put in trust for the sole use and benefit of his reputed wife Saskatchewan and their four children.[6] The records indicate that from 1823–32 payments were made to the family under "Freemen, deceased."

The Red River Settlement was attracting not only Scots and other immigrants, but also Roman Catholic and Church of England missionaries. After William Flett's death in November, an Anglican missionary baptized Saskatchewan and their four children. Saskatchewan was baptized "Isabella."

Beginning in the 1820s traders began to find white wives among the Red River settlers' families. This heralded a new era in the manners of the country. Native wives were no longer the customary marital choices of traders. Indeed they were rejected as unsuitable mates for officers and gentlemen.[7] If a white wife was unavailable, then Mixed-blood women were found to be more suitable.[8]

Flett's Journal at Edmonton House

Racism began with the arrival of white settlers and, in particular, with white women. The new arrivals, with their attitudes of racial, moral and social superiority, looked down upon the Native and Mixed-blood wives of traders. Sylvia Van Kirk writes:
In fact, the question of color became an issue for the first time. Traditionally, native wives, apart from the European names often bestowed upon them, had been referred to as "my woman", "the mother of my children", "the old lady" or "the guid wife", which revealed no concern for their racial origin.[9]

The derogatory word "squaw" began to be applied to Native wives. As well, white women saw Native and Mixed-blood women as potential rivals.[10] With the rise of racism, couples like Flett and Saskatchewan would find themselves more comfortable in Native, Métis and Mixed-blood surroundings than European. Despite a growing culture of racism, these brave and hardy men and women prepared the way for a new nation, carving it out of the wilderness around them.

CHAPTER 5

Saskatchewan: A Venerable Sojourner

IN WHICH WE ARE INTRODUCED AGAIN TO SASKATCHEWAN, NOW AN OLDER WOMAN, WHO IS CALLED UPON TO BRING HER ENERGY AND ABILITIES TO SUPPORT HER MOTHERLESS GRANDCHILDREN AS THEY JOIN WITH THEIR FATHER IN A PERILOUS AND HISTORIC JOURNEY WESTWARD.

SELDOM DO THE NATIVE WIVES OF TRADERS APPEAR IN the historical records of the day. In the journals and archives of trading companies, entries about Native women are few and fragmented. Our great-great-great grandmother Saskatchewan is listed only briefly in the Hudson's Bay Company's archival records. Her name is given as Saskatchewan in her husband, William Flett's, will. A year and a half after his death she was baptized "Isabella." Her death and burial is recorded thus: "Widow Flett aged 70 years listed in 'Burials at the Indian Church Red River', 26 October 1845." Finally, in a footnote, she appears in the Red River Census 1827–35, as living with a son-in-law, Robert Rowland on Lot 195 in the Red River Settlement. Rowland had married William Flett and Saskatchewan's eldest daughter Elizabeth (Betsy).[1]

These entries would have been the only record of Saskatchewan had it not been for the HBC's most flamboyant and successful Governor, George Simpson. Simpson was a Scot who took over the leadership of the Company in 1820. He was largely responsible for guiding the Company to the peak of its expan-

Saskatchewan: A Venerable Sojourner

sion when it controlled about 7.8 million square kilometres of territory, nearly a twelfth of the earth's land surface. His decisions as governor, and a brief mention of Saskatchewan in his journal, provide an insight into her life and her remarkable qualities. These qualities, I believe, she passed on to her granddaughter, and our great grandmother, Eliza Wishart.

Saskatchewan was among the first colonists from the Red River Settlement that the HBC sent in 1841 to settle in the Oregon Territory. The purpose of the emigration was to relieve the overpopulation in the Settlement. More important, the Company hoped settlement in the Pacific Northwest would strengthen the claims of the British to the Oregon territory; a permanent border had not yet been established between Britain and the United States.[2] Governor Simpson recognized that the occupation of the Oregon Territory by American settlers would jeopardize the HBC's valuable fur trade in that region and might result in the ultimate conquest of the land by the United States, which was currently held by a "joint occupation treaty."[3]

The Red River colonists were made up of 23 families, making a total of 121 people, of which 77 were children.[4] Apart from Saskatchewan, the contingent was composed of Mixed-blood and Métis. Saskatchewan was the oldest traveller and the only full-blooded Native.[5] She travelled with her son, William Flett Jr., and his four children, three daughters and one son, ranging in age from eleven to four. The list of colonists does not include Flett's wife, Margaret McNabb, who died in 1838 possibly after

> Oregon territory or Oregon Country covered a vast tract of land reaching from the Rocky Mountains to the Pacific Ocean and from the present-day boundaries of northern California to Alaska. The HBC's Columbia Department included all of the Oregon Country plus what is now northern British Columbia. Both the U.S. and Canada signed the Convention of Joint Occupancy in 1818 which gave equal rights of trade and settlement.

the birth of their fourth child.[6] For such an arduous trip, Saskatchewan likely filled the role of their surrogate mother. What makes her participation in this venture remarkable is that she was 66 years old.

Governor Simpson was known in fur trade circles as "the little emperor"; his hero was Napoleon.[7] He chose James Sinclair to lead the party. Sinclair was a Mixed-blood who had been educated at the University of Edinburgh.[8] He was also a man thoroughly acquainted with prairie travel. He was respected by Métis and Mixed-blood alike, who knew he could deal in a competent manner with any Natives met on the way.[9] He proved to be an excellent choice.

The colonists would travel 2,700 kilometres over some of the most difficult terrain imaginable and through territory previously unexplored by white men. Their destination was Oregon country. According to the plan they were to be placed at Cowlitz and Nisqually, HBC farms prepared for them at the southern end of Puget Sound near Fort Vancouver, now Vancouver, Washington.[10] The fort was the headquarters of the HBC in the Pacific Northwest from 1825 to 1849 and was established to reinforce the British claim to the coast.

On June 10, 1841, Sinclair gathered the party on the White Horse Plain, about 20 kilometres from the Red River Settlement. Each head of the family had been instructed to bring two or three Red River carts. The carts were ideal for travel on the plains. Built entirely of wood, usually oak, with one-and-a-half metre high wheels and an open box on top, they were tied together with buffalo hide that dried to a tight, strong binding. Carts could ford streams and be easily dismantled and made into a raft to cross rivers. Because they were made of wood, they were easily repaired. For protection against the elements they could be covered by canvas or buffalo hides. Driving a horse or an ox, and attaching a halter rope tied to other carts fore and aft, one driver could handle several carts.[11]

Fifty carts, 60 horses, 7 oxen and 3 English cows and countless dogs cut a wide, two-kilometre-long swath through the tall grass. The long, moving column undoubtedly sparkled with gaiety and a sense of adventure. The men and boys rode horseback, while the

Saskatchewan: A Venerable Sojourner

Half-breed's cart
GRAHAM AND DURKIN, GLENBOW ARCHIVES

women and children travelled in the slower moving horse-drawn carts seated on heaps of supplies. Peaking through the swirling dust, the travellers would catch glimpses of prairie roses and wood lilies.

To assist with the supplies which had to last into the summer and fall, the HBC advanced the settlers such essentials as pemmican, buffalo hides, blankets, tobacco, guns, shot, powder, flints and knives. Each party was to keep other items, such as cooking utensils, to a minimum. The men were to wear clothing used on buffalo hunts. This garb consisted of buckskin shirt and jacket, worn with homespun pants. Capotes, long cloaks usually with a hood, were carried for cold weather. Both men and women chose moccasins as the best protection against sore and blistered feet on the long journey.[12]

Like the other women and girls, Saskatchewan wore simple Red River clothing: dark homespun dresses and shawls, with bright kerchiefs worn on the head or around the throat or, if married, across the chest. Among the women, Saskatchewan sat tall despite her advanced years, her braided black hair falling over her back.

Sinclair organized the party the same way he did on the trails with the Métis. The HBC had appointed him leader with authority to use discipline if rules for travel were broken. The strictest discipline was to be observed if the trip over unknown country

What Lies Behind the Picture?

was to be completed safely. Fortunately, there were few, if any, inexperienced adult travellers in the party. The colonists knew how to camp efficiently; repair their carts and dismantle them if necessary to make rafts to negotiate rivers; build bridges over streams; handle horses; and hunt game to replenish their food supply. Some of the party brought along their best horses for chasing buffalo to secure meat should they run into a herd on the way. A few oxen were a safeguard against famine.

The colonists guarded their livestock carefully, night and day, for fear they would be lost or stolen by pilfering Native parties. In view of such dangers, they built a protective circle with their carts each night. A guard watched from sundown to sunrise.[13] The threats of Native attack, prairie fires, stampeding buffalo, frequent swarms of insects and dangerous river crossings were all part of the hardships they were to encounter as they left the comparative security of their Red River farms for an unknown future in an unknown land.

For the first part of the trip the colonists followed the trail that linked HBC posts at Fort Ellice, Fort Carlton, Fort Pitt and Fort Edmonton. Sixteen kilometres beyond Portage la Prairie, they followed the fork in the Assiniboine River that led to Fort Ellice, 320 kilometres from Fort Garry. Once there, they replenished stocks, repaired carts and took on fresh horses. Having journeyed through the tall grass of the Red River valley which reached to their horses' bellies, they entered aspen parkland and prairie grassland. Everywhere the grassland was dotted with fuzzy prairie crocus, bright yellow flowers of buffalo bean, yellow lady slippers, wild rose, and brilliant pinks and yellow of the milk vetches and loco weeds. In the morning they would awake to air laden with the scent of wild roses and wolf willow.

As they progressed they could not help but notice the singular beauty of the land—stands of wolf willow, Manitoba Maple, white birch, aspen and poplar; and flowers of saskatoons, currants, raspberries and cranberries. When they made brief stops their horses grazed on rough fescue grass as gophers (ground squirrels) darted here and there. Sharp-tailed grouse crouched

Saskatchewan: A Venerable Sojourner

Half-breeds travelling
PAUL KANE, ROYAL ONTARIO MUSEUM

in the buckbrush while overhead prairie hawks watched for prey. The colonists pushed onward through aspen parkland and what seemed like endless plains of prairie grass interrupted only by the sight of furtive coyotes stalking mice or wolves watching herds of grazing buffalo, waiting for the opportune moment to strike. Reaching the three-hundred-metre-wide and fast-running South Saskatchewan River, they put their supplies and carts on huge rafts and poled their way across, barely escaping disaster.

The trail led them through country where the powerful Blackfoot Confederacy[14] were pushing dangerously into Cree territory. The party wished to avoid the Blackfoot who were ancestral enemies of their relatives, the Cree. While the Red River carts were ideal for the level country of parkland and the prairies, the rubbing of rotating, wooden wheels on wooden hubs produced a high screeching sound that could be heard for miles around. The colonists were constantly on guard, fearful that the noise would alert hostile Natives long in advance of their approaching caravan.

Governor George Simpson, who was on a journey around

What Lies Behind the Picture?

the world, caught up to the party as they neared Fort Carlton, located on the south bank of the North Saskatchewan River. The most powerful man in British North America[15] had recently been honoured by the Queen with a knighthood. In March, 1841, he left London and crossed the Atlantic on the first leg of his journey, which would eventually take 19 months and 26 days.[16] Simpson travelled across Canada's great river highways, often at the rate of 160 kilometres a day, with the aid of his skilled Iroquois canoe men. He reached Fort Garry in early June and began the 1,500 kilometre journey to Fort Edmonton, catching up to the Sinclair party near Fort Carlton. In his journal he records:

Since we had fallen upon the trail of the emigrants, we could observe, by the number of their encampments, that we were marching at three or four times their pace. . . . From the information of Indians, we were looking out for these people; and accordingly, about two hours after starting, we gained a view of the lengthened cavalcade, winding its course over the plains. These emigrants consisted of agriculturists and others, principally natives of Red River settlement. There were twenty-three families, the heads being generally young and active, though a few of them were advanced in life, more particularly one poor woman, upwards of seventy-five years of age [more accurately 66 years of age], *who was tottering after her son to his new home. This venerable wanderer was a native of Saskatchewan, the name of which, in fact, she bore. She had been absent from this land of her birth for 18 years; and on catching the first glimpse of the river, from the hill near Carlton, she burst, under the influence of old recollections, into a violent flood of tears. During the two days that the party spent at the fort, she scarcely ever left the bank of the stream, appearing to regard it with as much veneration as the Hindoo* [sic] *regards the Ganges.*[17]

What were the emotions that lay behind our great-great-great grandmother's weeping? No one has recorded what Saskatchewan thought but one can imagine that a flood of memories from bygone days swept over her as she sat on the

Saskatchewan: A Venerable Sojourner

Governor General's party crossing Lake of the Woods
SYDNEY PRIOR, NATIONAL ARCHIVES OF CANADA, C-012861

bank of the river and cried copious tears. Did she miss her tribal sisters, many of whom were now dead? Did she recall the pain she felt in giving up her family and community to enter a world foreign to her when she became William Flett's country wife? Did she remember her struggle to make the transition from her Native ways to those more European? Amidst her tears, was she grateful that her husband had left money in trust for her and her four children?[18] Did she weep because she believed she would never see some of her own children and grandchildren again? We can only guess at the thoughts behind the tears of this time-honoured old woman.

As she arose and made her way back to the fort to rejoin the party, perhaps Saskatchewan realized she would never see this place again, and that her bones would be buried in a land far from her place of birth.

Governor Simpson continues his journal with these comments: *As a contrast to this superannuated daughter of the Saskatchewan, the band contained several young travelers, who had, in fact, made their appearances in this world since the commencement of the journey. Beyond this inevitable detention, which seldom exceeded a few hours, these inter-*

What Lies Behind the Picture?

esting events had never interfered with the progress of the brigade; and both mother and child used to jog on, as if jogging on were the condition of human existence.[19]

At least three of the overland colonist mothers had babies during the journey. Young mothers may not have been acquainted with Native birth practices while on the trail.[20] In such circumstances, Saskatchewan attended in the births and shared her knowledge of birthing.[21] Each family had two or three carts. In order to lighten the load on the horses drawing the carts, the women and children dismounted from time to time. To keep pace, they jogged along behind.

Simpson continues his observations of the colonists:

As they marched in single file, their cavalcade extended above a mile in length; and we increased the length of the column by marching in company. The emigrants were healthy and happy, living in the greatest abundance and enjoying the journey with high relish.

Before coming up to these people, we had seen evidence of the comfortable state of their commissariat in the shape of two or three still warm buffaloes, from which only the tongues and few other choice bits had been taken. This spectacle gave us hopes of soon seeing the animals ourselves; and accordingly it was not long before we saw our game on either side of the road, grazing and stalking about in bands of between twenty and a hundred, to the number of about five thousand in all.[22]

After enjoying one last but brisk buffalo hunt with some of Simpson's men, the Red River travellers replenished their stock of provisions, secured more horses and resumed their journey. While still in the company of Simpson's party, they halted at Turtle River for breakfast. Simpson writes:

In order to do honour to this day—the first occasion perhaps on which two large bands of civilized men had met as friends in these vast prairies—I put the men in high spirits with a dram, while a donation of wine, tea and sugar rendered the women the merriest and happiest gossips in the world.

Saskatchewan: A Venerable Sojourner

He continues his account:
The elders of this little congregation sat in council with Mr. Rowand [Chief Factor at Edmonton] *and myself on the subject of their route and various incidental matters . . . About three in the afternoon, we took leave of our fellow-travelers with mutual wishes for a prosperous journey.*[23]

For Saskatchewan and the rest of the party, it was now a matter of setting their faces steadfastly toward the most difficult and dangerous part of the trip.

CHAPTER 6

Journey into the Unknown

IN WHICH IS DESCRIBED A JOURNEY UNDER THE CONSTANT FEAR OF ATTACK. UPON REACHING FORT EDMONTON, THE RENOWNED NATIVE CHIEF MASKI-PITOON JOINS THE PARTY AS A GUIDE AND THEY CHART A COURSE THROUGH WOODLANDS, FOOTHILLS AND RUGGED MOUNTAIN TERRAIN.

A FIRST-HAND ACCOUNT OF THE PERILS OF THE JOURNEY survives. John Flett, likely a cousin of William Flett Jr.,[1] years later would describe the hardships and the hostility the Red River contingent met after their departure from Fort Carlton in July 1841.[2] William J. Betts, in an article, "From Red River to the Columbia," quotes John Flett:[3]

Dangers were now thickening around us. On the ground over which we were passing a great battle had been fought between the Cree and Blackfeet, the Crees being worsted. We kept men on guard day and night. War parties on every side. We now begin to believe what others had told us, that we should never get through. Still we forced our way on, and on the 10th of July crossed the Saskatchewan River to Fort Pitt. Here we found many wounded Crees, who had fled to the fort for protection. Here we rested for two days, and on the 12th again broke camp, traveling on the north side of the river until we reached Fort Edmonton on the twentieth, where we crossed the river.[4]

The arrival at Fort Edmonton aroused memories for

Journey into the Unknown

Saskatchewan and was something of a homecoming for William Flett Jr. His early boyhood was spent at the fort when his father William Flett Sr. served as Master and Canoe builder from 1814–1820.

The fort was surrounded by tall pickets and bastions with fortified gateways. Roughly hexagon in form, it was situated in a commanding position above an almost perpendicular part of the riverbank, which was about 60 metres in height. The buildings were smeared with red earth mixed with oil which produced a durable brown. John Rowand, whom the party had met on the trail, was the Chief Factor. Rowand ruled from a three-storey log mansion whose huge banquet hall—measuring 30 x 30 metres—was decorated with bright, gaudy colours and a variety of sculptures. Under Rowand, Fort Edmonton had become one of the most important HBC trading centres. Its value included the building of a large number of York boats, which had long since become the best means for carrying fur and trade goods to and from York Factory.

Here Sinclair met the famous Cree Chief Maski-pitoon known as Maskepetoon, Bras Croche or Broken Arm and baptized Abraham. He belonged to the Wetaskiwin band of Cree.[5] A year before Sinclair met him, the chief had been converted to Christianity by the Wesleyan missionary Robert T. Rundle. Before coming under the influence of Rundle, he had gained a reputation as a warrior with a violent temper. While a young man he was reputed to have scalped his wife Susewisk alive.[6] After his conversion, he was taught to read and write Cree syllabics by the missionary Thomas Woolsey.[7]

Maski-pitoon became a force for peace—seeking reconcilia-

Due to floods in 1825 and again in 1830, the fort was moved in 1831 from its location on the river bank on the north side of the river, near the present-day power plant, to higher ground, just below the present-day Alberta Legislative Buildings.

What Lies Behind the Picture?

Fort Edmonton
NATIONAL ARCHIVES OF CANADA

tion with enemy tribes. Although a Blackfoot killed his father, Maski-pitoon forgave the killer and presented him with a chief's costume. According to Egerton Ryerson Young, a Methodist missionary, Maski-pitoon "was a magnificent looking man physically, and was keen and intelligent."[8] He was to become an invaluable guide for Sinclair and his party.

At Fort Edmonton the party rested and replenished their supplies in preparation for what was to be the next hazardous leg of the journey. Crossing the North Saskatchewan by ferry the party left behind the woodlands and followed a trail southward between the Whitemud and Blackmud Creeks and once again into lovely parkland with its bluffs of trees, expansive skies and rolling landscape.

John Flett's account continues:

We traveled far out of our direct route for safety, but now we faced unknown dangers. The region through which we had to pass was fine hunting ground, buffalo being very plentiful, and the different tribes—Blackfeet, Assiniboines, Peigans, Crees—were continuously striving for it, many bloody battles being fought.[9]

Journey into the Unknown

They skirted Gull Lake for fear of dangerous encounters and crossed the little Red Deer or the Red Deer River at Red Deer Crossing, which was used by both Cree and Blackfoot as they travelled north and south to trade, fight or visit with other tribes.[10] John Flett continues as follows:

Moving southward through this region, keeping careful watch for hostiles, we again reached the waters of the south branch on the 30th of July . . . While out hunting we [John Flett and his younger brother] *were surrounded by hostile Indians. We concealed ourselves until dark. . . . Having stripped off our outer clothing, we fastened it on our horses and plunged in. The water was cold, icy cold, the river was very swift and about two hundred yards wide. Twice we swam the river, and after wandering about for two days at last reached camp and safety. Of all the dangers I have seen in pioneer life of fifty years, the dangers of those two days were the worst. We overtook our party encamped at old Fort McLeod, an abandoned post of the H.B.Co., now known as the British Pas, or Rocky Mountain. Here we were compelled to abandon our carts and pack our goods on the back of oxen and horses. After a long debate about what should be taken and what should be left behind, we at last had our train in readiness, and again started on our way.*

At this point in his account Flett departs from the serious danger he and his younger brother had experienced to describe what happened as they made the transition from carts to oxen and horses. I pick up his colourful account as all hell broke loose:

The oxen, however, were unused to the mode of traveling, and, becoming frightened, a stampede ensued. Then what a sight—oxen bellowing, kicking, running; horses neighing, raring, plunging; children squalling; women crying; men swearing, shouting and laughing; while the air seemed full of blankets, kettles, sacks of pots, pans and jerkied buffalo [dried meat]. *At last the cattle were again secured. All our goods that could be found were gathered up, and the remnants repacked, and we started.*[11]

What Lies Behind the Picture?

Fort Edmonton, 1860
ELLA WALKER, CITY OF EDMONTON ARCHIVES

Journey into the Unknown

What Lies Behind the Picture?

Sinclair's party quickly adapted to the new mode of travel. Under Maski-pitoon's guidance, they headed into the Canadian Rockies. Governor Simpson had instructed them to approach the mountains by way of Jasper House, located on the north bank of the Athabasca River, across from the entrance to what is now Jasper National Park. They were then to cross the mountains by way of the Athabasca Pass to the Boat Encampment near the Columbia River. From there, they were to float down the treacherous Columbia River system.[12] Sinclair, likely in consultation with Maski-pitoon, had other plans. Instead of turning northwest he headed southwest. The decision to disobey Simpson and remain on horseback until reaching Oregon Territory may have saved many lives. In 1846, five years later, the HBC had recorded 61 deaths by drowning in the Columbia River's torrential waters. Saskatchewan and the Red River emigrants had good reason to be thankful Sinclair was their leader and Maski-pitoon their guide.

Angling westward through the Little Red Deer Valley, they left the rolling foothills behind and made their way through cottonwoods which cast their welcoming shadow along the river floodplains. Nestling in the coulees were saskatoons, roses and fragrant bergamot, delicate blue flax and buckbrush. They then went through an opening in the Rocky Mountains called the Devil's Gap. Once through the gap they entered a wide valley with four glistening, greenish-blue lakes which reflected the lofty precipices and rugged mountains surrounding them. The largest was the leaf-shaped Minnewanka, known to the Assiniboine as Minnee-wah-kah, the Lake Where the Spirits Dwell, located 15 kilometres from present-day Banff. After the party rested briefly on the eastern shores of the lakes, they made their way through a picturesque gorge following what is today known as Carrot Creek to the valley of the Bow River. Once the river was forded, they led their horses up and through a rocky incline called Whiteman's Gap, above present-day Canmore, Alberta. Here they entered what are now called the Spray Lakes and the Spray River Valley where they were surrounded by majestic and awe-inspiring peaks. Aspen, poplar and larch, against a green background of

Journey into the Unknown

lodgepole pine and spruce, were beginning to show tinges of their golden and orange fall colors. In the valleys the travellers made their way through a splurge of alpine flowers—Indian paint brush, columbine, lupine; and berry patches of saskatoons, wild raspberries and strawberries, chokecherries, and red elderberries. They would see deer, elk and bear, all familiar to prairie travellers, but as they ascended higher up they saw the unfamiliar mountain sheep and mountain goats grazing on grassy mountain slopes. Following Whiteman's Creek they crossed a height of land which passed between snow-capped mountain peaks. The descending waters of the creek led them to the top of the Great Divide. In the distance, standing over 3,600 metres high, was Mount Assiniboine and its glistening glacier. As they began their long descent, moving westward on the present-day British Columbia side, Maski-pitoon guided them through passes unknown to Europeans, which later became designated as White Man Pass, Sinclair Canyon or Red Rock Gorge, and Sinclair Pass.[13]

With James Sinclair and Maski-pitoon as pathfinders, the party crossed the Canadian plains at a time when the Cree were at war with the Blackfoot Confederacy. Men, women and children, some less than three months old, and Saskatchewan in her sixties, travelled across some of the most difficult mountain terrain in North America. They then entered the Oregon Territory still in constant danger of attack. After almost five months the group arrived at Fort Vancouver, the Hudson's Bay Company's great western depot.[14] Remarkably, they had crossed half a continent between Fort Garry and the Pacific Ocean without the loss of the life of a single member of the party. That they did so, in the words of Geneva Lent is "little less than miraculous and is surely unequalled in the pioneer history of this continent."[15]

SINCLAIR'S SETTLERS EXPECTED A WARM WELCOME AT Fort Vancouver. They were disappointed. From the outset, the HBC evaded its promise to place the Red River people on the farms it had promised to them. The contract seemed to be sidetracked. The travellers became restless. After many weeks of

What Lies Behind the Picture?

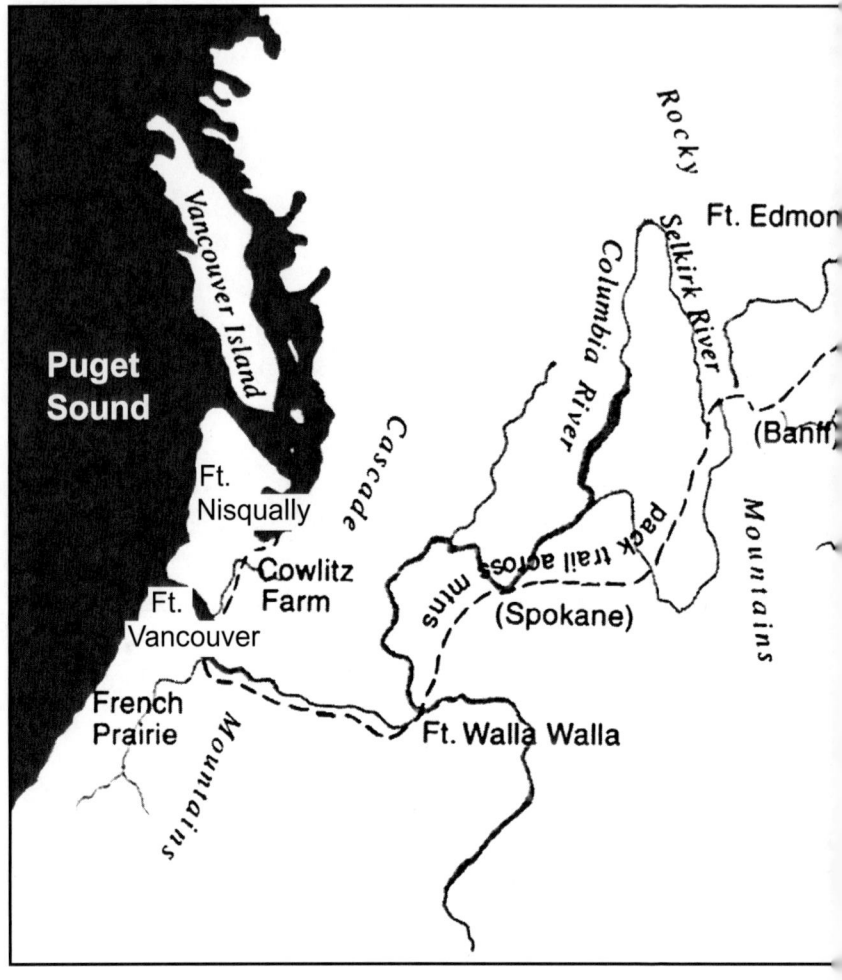

Overland to the Columbia
CHILDREN OF THE FUR TRADE, MOUNTAIN PRESS

waiting at the fort, some of the party were placed on farms at Cowlitz and Nisqually, but under conditions that were to prove disheartening. It was not a promising end to the hardships the party had endured in making its long journey to settle in new homes. His task accomplished, Sinclair left the party to rejoin his family in Red River. He departed believing an injustice had been done to the people he had led in good faith to the Oregon. He had come to know them well as they followed him across the continent.[16]

Journey into the Unknown

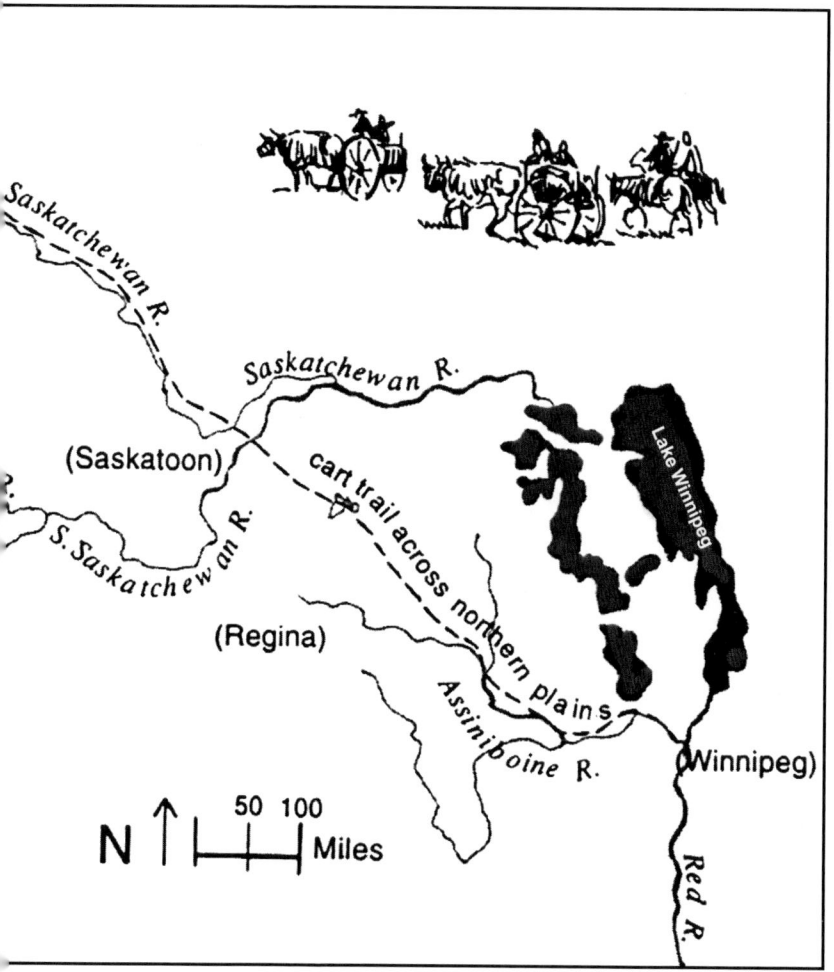

When crops failed at Nisqually, Chief Factor McLoughlin agreed to release the settlers from their contract entirely if they moved to the Willamette Valley and became independent farmers. This would remove them from any further obligation to the HBC.[17] Flett and others moved either to the lower Willamette Valley or the north Tualatin Plains.

The influx of American settlers over the Oregon trail tested the Red River families to the core. Many Americans who came west had high expectations, and resented finding Métis and

What Lies Behind the Picture?

Mixed-blood on choice land. John Jackson describes the emerging ethos: "It was hard to ignore the whispers, the malicious laughs behind a hand, or dark glances in the store."[18] Increasing social pressure resulted in many of the Métis and Mixed-blood moving to more marginal areas. The U.S. census of 1850, which asked detailed questions about race, place of origin, family, and occupation, indicated that Oregon had a population of 13,294 people. Jackson notes that, "Indian parentage was recorded only if an individual was prepared to share that fact, and a check of the Red River people reveals that they were not forward about a potential social embarrassment."[19] Some were so sensitive about their Native heritage that they never spoke of it.

A core of French-speaking Catholic Métis in the Willamette Valley held on to their settlement. With established Catholic churches as their base, this community was able to resist the social pressure of the prevailing culture.[20] Others were not so fortunate. The struggle to adapt to such pressure and racial discrimination resulted in many giving up the struggle. Some Métis, because of their Native heritage, became official Indians and settled on Indian Reservations. Tragically many of the Pacific Northwest Métis suppressed their identity.[21]

Mixed-blood families faced the same dilemma. They could assimilate with the dominant white culture or run away from it. If they tried to pass themselves off as white, as many did, they faced the risk that their Native background would follow like an inescapable shadow.

Racism was not new to Saskatchewan. While living in the Red River settlement, she had experienced the racist attitudes of the white wives of traders, of Governor George Simpson and many of his staff. She would not be surprised that such attitudes reached into the Pacific Northwest.

A few Mixed-blood settlers, like John Flett, found employment in government service. Flett served as an interpreter because he was trusted by the Natives in their negotiations with Indian Commissioners. He was disturbed, however, by the callous treatment the Native people were receiving. During his time in Indian service, Flett watched as the last of the Natives were

Journey into the Unknown

placed on reserves where they suffered cultural disintegration and poverty. The painful process of Indian dispossession compelled John Flett to try to lessen the terrible impact.[22] He finally settled upon land only a few miles from Fort Nisqually where he died on December 12, 1892, by all accounts a grand old man liked by all who knew him.

William Flett Jr.'s time in the Pacific Northwest had quite a different ending. Sometime after his arrival in the Pacific Northwest, he married Mary Curtnir, who was about his same age.[23] They had a daughter who was baptized in 1845.[24] After leaving Nisqually, Flett settled with his family on the Tualatin Plains of Oregon. The discovery of gold in California in 1848 attracted William Flett Jr. and many Oregon settlers. A group of about 150 assembled in Oregon City. They were guided south through dangerous Native territory to the gold fields in the Sacramento area. Disaster awaited the prospective miners. Less resistant to disease than their American neighbours, the Red River party had little immunity to cholera and other diseases that were ravaging the camps of the gold-seekers. It was reported that 80 out of the Oregon company died of scurvy or diarrhea. Those who died included William Flett Jr.[25]

And what of Saskatchewan? It would seem unlikely that she would make the long, arduous and dangerous journey back to the Red River Settlement. Nevertheless, she did. With her son's marriage to Mary Curtnir, she was no longer needed to fill the role of mother to his children. The way was open for her to return to the place where her husband was buried and her remaining family lived.

James Sinclair, after waiting out the winter, joined the first HBC brigade bound from Fort Colville, southwest of modern Spokane, up the Columbia River to the Boat Encampment. Sinclair probably took Saskatchewan with him because of her experience and usefulness on the trail, not to mention her remarkable stamina. The trip up river meant a month of hard labour over treacherous waters. At the Boat Encampment, Sinclair and Saskatchewan joined a Company pack train and crossed the mountains through Athabasca Pass. The Pass was a perilous descent of 500 metres over

What Lies Behind the Picture?

a distance of 50 kilometres as it followed the swollen Whirlpool River. With the spring rains, they found themselves dripping wet and wading through numerous fords and swollen streams. The Pass, which had claimed many lives by drowning, was not without its beauty. They had remarkable views of ice fields, glaciers and wildlife; and the mountain that would later be named Edith Cavell, stood more than 3,000 meters high. Reaching the Athabasca River safely, they continued by boat brigade to Jasper House; and then on to Fort Edmonton by cart brigade. Here they joined the earliest boat or cart brigade for Fort Garry where Sinclair rejoined his family, and resumed trading.[26] As for Saskatchewan, she completed her remarkable journey by returning to her remaining family in the Red River Settlement and the place where her husband was buried.

The Hudson's Bay Company archives record that she died at the age of 70 and was buried in the cemetery of the Indian Church Red River on October 26, 1845.[27] This is confirmed in the early registers of burials in the churchyard cemetery surrounding St. Peter's Church, which also indicate she was living in the Indian settlement of St. Peter (Dynevor),[28] four years after the historic journey and her return from the Pacific Northwest.

Saskatchewan lived 22 years longer than her husband. Though William Flett and Saskatchewan had shared a life in the woodlands and on the plains, rivers and lakes of a vast northern landscape, they did not share the same gravesite. At the end, were they separated because she was Native? How sad that this woman who, like so many of her Native sisters, was so vital to the Hudson's Bay Company's fur trade, did not share the resting place of her husband. He was buried in the churchyard of St. John's Cathedral, designated as the Hudson's Bay Company cemetery.

In September 1846, a year after her death, news arrived that the U.S.–Canada boundary had been set at 49 degrees north latitude.[29] Saskatchewan's return meant she was buried in a Native cemetery in Rupert's Land. I hope this remarkable woman was lovingly laid to rest by her children and grandchildren.

Journey into the Unknown

St. Peter's Church (Dynevor) and Indian graveyard
RUPERT'S LAND COLLECTION, ARCHIVES OF MANITOBA

THE WISHARTS

CHAPTER 7

Thomas Wishart: Adventure by the Sea

WHEREIN WE ARE INTRODUCED TO THOMAS WISHART AND HIS ADVENTURES AT SEA AS HE JOURNEYS TO HIS NEW HOME ON THE RED RIVER IN RUPERT'S LAND.

On Sunday, May 22, 1819, at the age of 23, Thomas Wishart, our great-great-grandfather,[1] signed on with the HBC as a labourer for a term of five years and a salary of £20 per annum. He was not the first Orcadian Wishart to do so. Among the first to sign on with the HBC was Nicholas Wishart also from Orkney. He joined the Company as a tailor in 1776. Frequent mention is made of him "making clothing for men." In 1784 it is recorded that he was "lost in the Barren grounds [the prairies] and devoured by wolves."[2]

Thomas boarded the HBC ship the *Prince of Wales* at Gravesend on the Thames, England.[3] Quite coincidentally, there was on board the ship a short, stout, and balding man, John Franklin, who had booked passage through the HBC and was to become, in his lifetime, larger than life.[4]

Following the end of the Napoleonic Wars in 1815, the British Admiralty turned its attention to Arctic exploration and renewed efforts to discover the Northwest Passage to China. As well, the Admiralty hoped to advance scientific knowledge of the Arctic and its sea.[5] For this formidable task, they chose John

Thomas Wishart: Adventure by the Sea

Franklin, an experienced naval man and a competent naturalist, and William Edward Parry, the well-know explorer of polar waters. Franklin was to journey overland to search for the Northwest Passage, and Parry was to explore by sea.[6]

Unlike Franklin, Wishart's presence in England is a mystery. Perhaps he was pressed into military service during the Napoleonic Wars of 1793 to 1815. Orkney seamen were vulnerable to "press gangs." Some 1,500 to 2,000 men volunteered or were pressed into the service of the Royal Navy, while others served in locally-raised regiments for defence against invasion.[7] Wishart, like many Orkney men, had experienced the sea as a fisherman, so it is possible that he served in the British Navy. With the defeat of France, most able-bodied seamen were discharged. At some point, following his tenure, he decided to become an adventurer and embrace a different way of life. He signed on with the HBC.

Leaving Gravesend, the *Prince of Wales,* with its consorts the *Eddystone* and the *Wear,* charted a course up the east coast of England to Orkney.[8] On June 3, 1819, it rounded the rocky shoreline and passed a bold protruding rock called Johny Groat's House. Shortly after, a pilot came from the main shore of Scotland and steered the ships between the different islands to the outer anchorage at Stromness.[9] As they entered the harbour, cannon fire from the port announced the arrival of the ships. It was a signal for great excitement and activity. While the crews were engaged in taking on supplies and fresh water, sturdy new recruits were registered and signed on board.

Franklin wanted to hire some Orkney boatmen for his expedition to the Arctic. It was difficult to procure men, however, even for the service of the HBC, due to the increased demand for boatmen for the herring fishery which had recently been established on the shores of the islands.[10]

Two weeks later, the *Prince of Wales* with the *Eddystone,* the *Wear* and the *Harmony,* a Moravian Missionary Society ship, began the journey to Hudson Bay. The *Harmony* headed for the Society's settlement on the coast of Labrador. Among the passengers on the other ships were Highland crofters recruited by Lord Selkirk for his settlement at the forks of the Red and

Assiniboine rivers. As the ships began the arduous two-and-a-half-month journey to York Factory, wives, families, sweethearts and well-wishers lined the dock to wave tearful goodbyes.

Wishart watched his homeland recede in the distance. Had he known the hardships and dangers that lay ahead, he might have returned to the family croft, joined the herring fishermen and died on Orkney soil.

At first the progress of the ships was slow because of the northwest wind and "much sea."[11] Early in July, however, they advanced rapidly westward and on the 25th they reached Davis Strait, between Greenland and Baffin Island. What a visual experience it must have been for Thomas—a maze of drifting icebergs and a crystalline world of intense colors, blazing white, indigo blue and emerald green. John Ross, among the first of naval explorers, wrote in his journal: "It is hardly possible to imagine anything more exquisite . . . by night as well as by day they [icebergs] glitter with a vividness of colour beyond the power of art to represent."[12]

The splendor of the eastern Arctic gave way to its dangers. As the ships made their way toward Hudson Strait, which leads into Hudson Bay, they were suddenly enveloped in fog and a heavy stream of ice. The *Prince of Wales* received several severe blows from the ice.[13] A few days later, the ship was surrounded by several large icebergs and had to proceed on a zigzag course in order to avoid being crushed. During the morning of August 7th, lookouts saw Resolution Island through the haze. It disappeared quickly behind a dense fog. Franklin records the following in his journal:

> [At] *"half-past twelve . . . we had the alarming view of barren rugged shore within a few yards towering over the mastheads. Almost instantly afterward, the ship struck violently on a point of rocks projecting from the island; and the ships side was brought so near to the shore that poles were prepared to push her off . . . the current hurried us along in contact with the rocky shore, and the prospect was alarming . . . there now seemed no possibility of escaping shipwreck. . . ."*[14]

Thomas Wishart: Adventure by the Sea

A sudden breeze came to their rescue. It seemed to be carrying them to safety, when suddenly the current forced them against a large iceberg lying aground. Franklin writes, "Our prospect was now more alarming than at any preceding period; and it would be difficult for me to portray the anxiety and dismay on the countenance of female passengers and children..."[15]

George Back, a midshipman, describes more vividly in his journal the alarm among the women and children:

... these poor creatures whose occupations were entirely on the shore and consequently were unused to such spectacles as they had just witnessed—uttered the most pious exclamations—fearing the torment of sudden death or the more horrible state of starvation—the screams of the children and the agonizing looks of despair of the fathers—with the hustle and confusion of the seamen added an awfulness to the scene which will never be obliterated from my memory.[16]

Miraculously, they escaped. The ship, however, received a blow that caused a serious leak. Crew and passengers frantically manned the pumps and everyone, including the women, began bailing water. Their efforts seemed in vain. Expecting the ship to sink, the crew sent women and children to the *Eddystone*. As a last desperate measure, a sail covered with oakum [loose fibers from old rope] was placed under the bottom of the ship. This caused the water going into the hold to lessen long enough for the damage to be brought under control. Midshipman Back writes, "We then assembled in the cabin where Lieutenant Franklin read prayers and returned thanks for the providential manner in which we have been saved."[17] Thomas Wishart shared those moments of anxiety and fear with the crew and passengers. He likely wondered if he would ever reach the safety of York Factory.

The dangers of Arctic waters were a new experience for him, but he was also about to encounter the people of this northern clime for the first time in his life. As the *Prince of Wales* and the *Eddystone* made their way along Hudson Strait, they steered near the shore to give the inhabitants, the Esquimaux [Inuit],

What Lies Behind the Picture?

the opportunity to barter.[18] (The *Wear* was presumed lost or shipwrecked but reappeared later.) Franklin describes the meeting, "... before noon about forty canoes, each holding one man, were assembled around the two ships. In the afternoon, when we approached nearer to the shore, five or six larger ones, containing the women and children came up."[19]

The Inuit's principal items for barter were oil [likely whale oil], sea-horse teeth [walrus teeth], whalebone, seal skin dresses, caps and boots, deer [caribou] skins and models of their canoes. The women brought figures of men, women, birds and other animals "carved with labour and ingenuity of sea-horse teeth."[20] They were very eager traders, more so than the men, "a button was sufficient to create the greatest joy—but a needle or a piece of old iron hoop seemed the most sought for."[21]

The 1819 voyage was likely Wishart's first experience of barter, a practice he would become more thoroughly acquainted with in the environs of York Factory. The features, dress and manners of this northern people would arouse his curiosity. Franklin's journal gives us some idea of what met Wishart's gaze. He says of the Inuit:

> *Their faces were broad and flat, the eyes small. The men were in general stout* [well built]. *Some of the younger women and children had rather pleasing countenances...*[22] *the men's dresses consisted of a jacket of seal-skin, the trousers of bear-skin, and several had caps of the white fox-skin. The female dresses were made of the same materials, but differently shaped, having a hood in which the infants were carried. We thought their manner very lively and agreeable. They were fond of mimicking our speech and gestures; but nothing afforded them greater amusement than when we attempted to retaliate by pronouncing any of their words.*[23]

After two and a half months of often harrowing travel, what a relief it must have been for Wishart, as well as the crew and the passengers, when the *Prince of Wales,* the *Eddystone* and the *Wear* were able to shape their course across Hudson Bay and arrive at York Factory to a gun salute.

Thomas Wishart: Adventure by the Sea

York Factory
HBC ARCHIVES, ARCHIVES OF MANITOBA

CHAPTER 8

Journey Inland

IN WHICH YORK FACTORY IS DESCRIBED AND JOHN FRANKLIN DESCRIBES THE RISKS, DANGERS AND HARDSHIPS FACED BY THOMAS WISHART AND OTHER MEMBERS OF THE BOAT BRIGADES AS THEY TRAVELLED INLAND, AS WELL AS THE STARK BEAUTY OF THE SCENERY.

THE SIGHT OF THE FORT MAY HAVE DAMPENED THE excitement caused by landing safely. It was located on the southwest shores of Hudson Bay on a narrow, marshy peninsula which separated two rivers, the Hayes and the Nelson. This was a mosquito-infested spot in the summer and an intensely cold place in the winter. Life for its residents was less than comfortable.

The surrounding country was flat and swampy without trees. Poplar, birch, larch and spruce trees, ordinarily available in the near vicinity, had been cut down for fuel.[1] Surrounding the fort was a stockade over six metres high. Inside the wall were two-storey main buildings: the residences of the governor and the HBC officers, and the single men's quarters. Nearby were warehouses for the storing of fur and trade goods. Small dwellings outside the main buildings housed married servants and their families. In the centre of the stockade stood a tall flagstaff with the Company's ensign of four beaver and a red cross.[2]

Of all the activities carried on at York Factory, perhaps none proved more astonishing to a newcomer like Wishart than the

Journey Inland

trade in skins. The inland brigades brought enormous numbers of beaver, muskrats, marten, fox, wolf and bear skins to the fort each summer. Tens of thousands of pelts of fur had to be readied for the long voyage to Gravesend, where they would be sold at the Company's London auctions.[3]

In his brief time at York Factory, Thomas Wishart learned what massive amounts of organization were necessary to trade with Native people to maximum benefit. It would be hard to escape the conclusion that the relationship between the Natives and Europeans was almost entirely based on the fur trade, and that the HBC administered its territory primarily for the exploitation of resources.

Wishart followed the route already taken by my other ancestors, Isaac Batt, James Spence and William Flett, as well as other HBC employees. He discovered, as did his predecessors, that travel inland from York Factory by boat upstream, was exhausting and dangerous. Men died on these journeys. The leading causes of death during portages to avoid falls, rapids or other water hazards, were drowning and strangulated hernias while carrying huge bundles of cargo.

Franklin, on witnessing for the first time the labour and risks involved with river travel, wrote:

It is not easy for any but an eye-witness to form an adequate idea of the exertion of the Orkney boatmen. . . . The necessity they are under frequently jumping into the water to lift boats over rocks, compels them to remain the whole day in wet clothes, at a season when the temperature is far below the freezing point. The immense loads, which they carry over portages, is not a [greater] *matter of surprise than the alacrity with which they perform these laborious duties.*[4]

From York Factory, Franklin's party, soon to be accompanied by HBC boats, travelled up the Hayes River. Although treacherous and rocky in places, its depth was suitable for the heavily-laden York boats. Almost from the beginning, tracking was required, that is, dragging the boat by a line to which the men on shore were harnessed. Upstream the work was more difficult and often more perilous. If Thomas could take his eyes off the

What Lies Behind the Picture?

sweeping motion of the five metre oars, he saw the beautiful scenery on the shoreline. Franklin described the effect of fall on the foliage:

> ... light yellow of fading poplars formed a fine contrast to the dark evergreen of the spruce, whilst the willows of an intermediate hue, served to shade the two principal masses of colour into each other. This scene was occasionally enlivened by the bright purple tints of the dogwood, blended with the browner shades of the dwarf birch, and frequently intermixed with the gay yellow flowers of the shrubby cinquefoil.[5]

With the prospect of winter descending, the party hurried on. They repeated the routine when necessary: emptying the boats, carrying, and restoring the cargo. Franklin wrote in his journal, "the setting sun threw the richest tints over the scene that I remember ever to have witnessed."[6] He also made note of the continued hardships the boatmen were experiencing; the rocks which formed the bed of the river at Knife Portage, were so sharp that "the feet of the boatmen are much lacerated."[7]

They reached Oxford House, a HBC trading post on Holey Lake, now Oxford Lake, on September 28. Here they found several Native tents whose occupants were ill with whooping cough. They listened to the incessant barking of a large number of dogs kept for dragging sleighs loaded with provisions and furs in winter.[8]

Further on they came to John Moore's Island where the Hayes River ran with tremendous force through channels formed by two rocky islands. It was here Wishart learned from the other boatmen that the previous year one of the men had a line break as he was hauling a boat up one of the channels. He slipped and fell into the water and was carried down the cascade. Every effort to save him had failed. His body was recovered and buried near the spot of his accident.[9]

On October 1, they came to Hill Gates Portage, where the river was swift and extremely narrow. Cliff walls rose 60 to 80 feet, hemming in the river so much that there was barely enough space for the men to use their oars. After navigating this narrow

Journey Inland

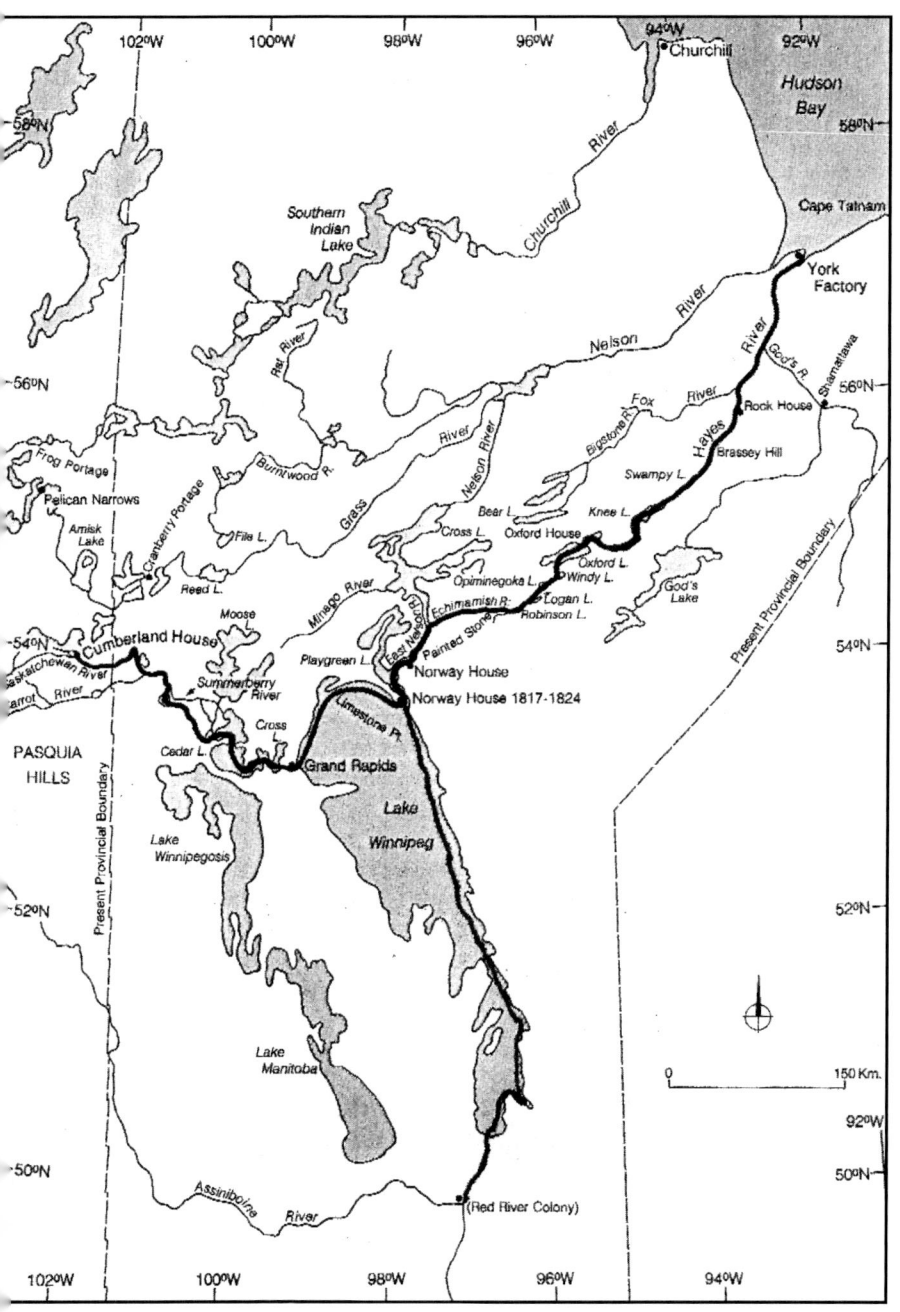

York Factory to Cumberland House
GEORGE BLACK, MCGILL-QUEENS UNIVERSITY PRESS

What Lies Behind the Picture?

stretch of water, they had to make treacherous portages at Upper and Lower Gate Portages. Finally, they arrived at White Fall Lake and entered its river, arriving at White Falls an hour after sunset.[10] By now Wishart was accustomed to exhaustion after a day's work, rolling himself in his blanket for a few hours of much-needed rest.

The boat brigade pushed ever onward, often encountering snow and rain. After another strenuous portage, Franklin wrote:
I shall long remember the rude and characteristic wildness of the scenery which surrounded these falls; rocks piled on rocks hung in rude and shapeless masses over the agitated torrents which swept their bases, whilst the bright and variegated tints of the mosses and lichens that covered the face of the cliffs, contrasting with the dark green of the pines which crowned their summits, added both beauty and grandeur to the scene.[11]

While walking on rocks near a falls, and undoubtedly enjoying the scenery, Franklin slipped and fell into the river. He was carried rapidly down stream and, after many failed attempts to gain a landing, he grasped hold of a willow. Two Company men in a boat came to his rescue. Fortunately, he was not hurt.[12]

In early October, they reached Norway House, located on the north east corner of Lake Winnipeg.[13] They were greeted warmly by the Lord Selkirk colonists who were on their way to the Selkirk Colony. They had shared the adventurous crossing of the Atlantic to York Factory and had departed from the fort a day before the Company men and Franklin's party.[14]

Upon arrival at Lake Winnipeg, a relieved Wishart knew the journey's end was near.

At Lake Winnipeg, which in Cree means "muddy waters," Franklin's expedition and many of the HBC boats journeyed inland while the remainder made their way up Lake Winnipeg to Fort Garry. Those going inland followed the north shore of Lake Winnipeg to the Grand Rapids and the North Saskatchewan River. The Company boats pushed on to Cumberland House and then to the various HBC posts before the onslaught of winter.

By early November, winter was setting in, and the rivers were

Journey Inland

freezing over. Franklin decided to winter over at Cumberland House before proceeding northward to the Coppermine River, where he built Fort Enterprise. With Fort Enterprise as his base, Franklin continued to the Arctic coastline in a disastrous trip interrupted by starvation, murder and the loss of 11 men. For all his difficulties Franklin became the first to survey thousands of kilometres of Arctic shoreline previously unknown to European explorers—a truly remarkable accomplishment in an unforgiving land that would one day take his life.[15]

On July 14, 1822, he returned to York Factory where he recorded that he had travelled 10,000 kilometres into "the heart of despair, the extremities of human suffering and death."[16]

Thomas Wishart began a different kind of life when he arrived at Fort Garry, a newcomer with faith in the future.

CHAPTER 9

Thomas and Barbara

WHEREIN IS RELATED THOMAS WISHART'S ARRIVAL AT A WATERSHED IN THE FUR TRADE WARS RESULTING IN HIS EMPLOYMENT IN THE STRUGGLING SELKIRK COLONY; AND HIS MARRIAGE TO BARBARA SPENCE, OUR GREAT-GREAT-GRANDMOTHER.

ALTHOUGH THOMAS WISHART SIGNED ON WITH THE HBC, his service to the Company did not last long, if it happened at all. By 1819, the time of his arrival at Red River, the North West Company and the Hudson's Bay Company recognized that their fur trade competition was becoming prohibitively costly, and violent. Over the years they had engaged in a constant battle over land and water and neither party was willing to give in.

At the centre of the strife was Lord Selkirk's Colony. The North West Company saw it as a threat to its main supply route. The colony had barely survived attempts in 1815 to destroy it by the Nor' Westers and their Métis allies who scattered the farmers and trampled their fields. At the Battle of Seven Oaks in 1816, the governor of the colony and 19 of his infantry were massacred by the Métis. On the open plain, the defenders of the colony were helpless before the mounted marksmen of the buffalo hunt.[1]

In the following summer of 1817, Selkirk reached the colony he had founded and the colonists were returned once more.

Thomas and Barbara

Ravaged seed plots were restored and crops sown. The Métis came to see the colony as a place where they, too, could settle, and as a market for the produce from their hunt.[2]

In 1819, the fur trading companies recognized that some sort of commercial union was necessary. The financial affairs of the NWC were in bad shape and morale was low. Furthermore, the Napoleonic Wars had hurt sales to the European markets for both companies. A union would stop the frequent clashes and expensive court battles, and it would eliminate costly competition and stabilize prices in the fur trade. A monopoly would be in the best interests of both trading companies. Whether this merger would serve the Native peoples' interests was another matter.[3]

The parties reached a final agreement in 1821. It had to be accepted by the British government, and translated into legislation, a process that took another year. With the amalgamation, the North West Company passed out of existence. Thus ended the vigorous, sometimes violent struggle for control of the hugely lucrative fur trade.

Thomas Wishart arrived during this tide in the affairs of the fur trade. He caught it at its flood, but it did not lead him to fame and fortune.

With the union, the Hudson's Bay Company hired George Simpson to manage what was now a vast enterprise. By most accounts, he was a dominating, often ruthless man, but considered by some to be a genius. Immediately after the union, Simpson directed his efforts to the badly needed rehabilitation of the fur trade so crippled by strife.[4] First, he cut down the number of outposts and employees. Relying on the best of the HBC

> In 1824, the HBC acting for Lord Selkirk was entrusted with the colony. During this period it became more commonly known as the Red River Settlement. In 1834 the HBC purchased the colony and in 1835 a Council was appointed to govern the settlement.

What Lies Behind the Picture?

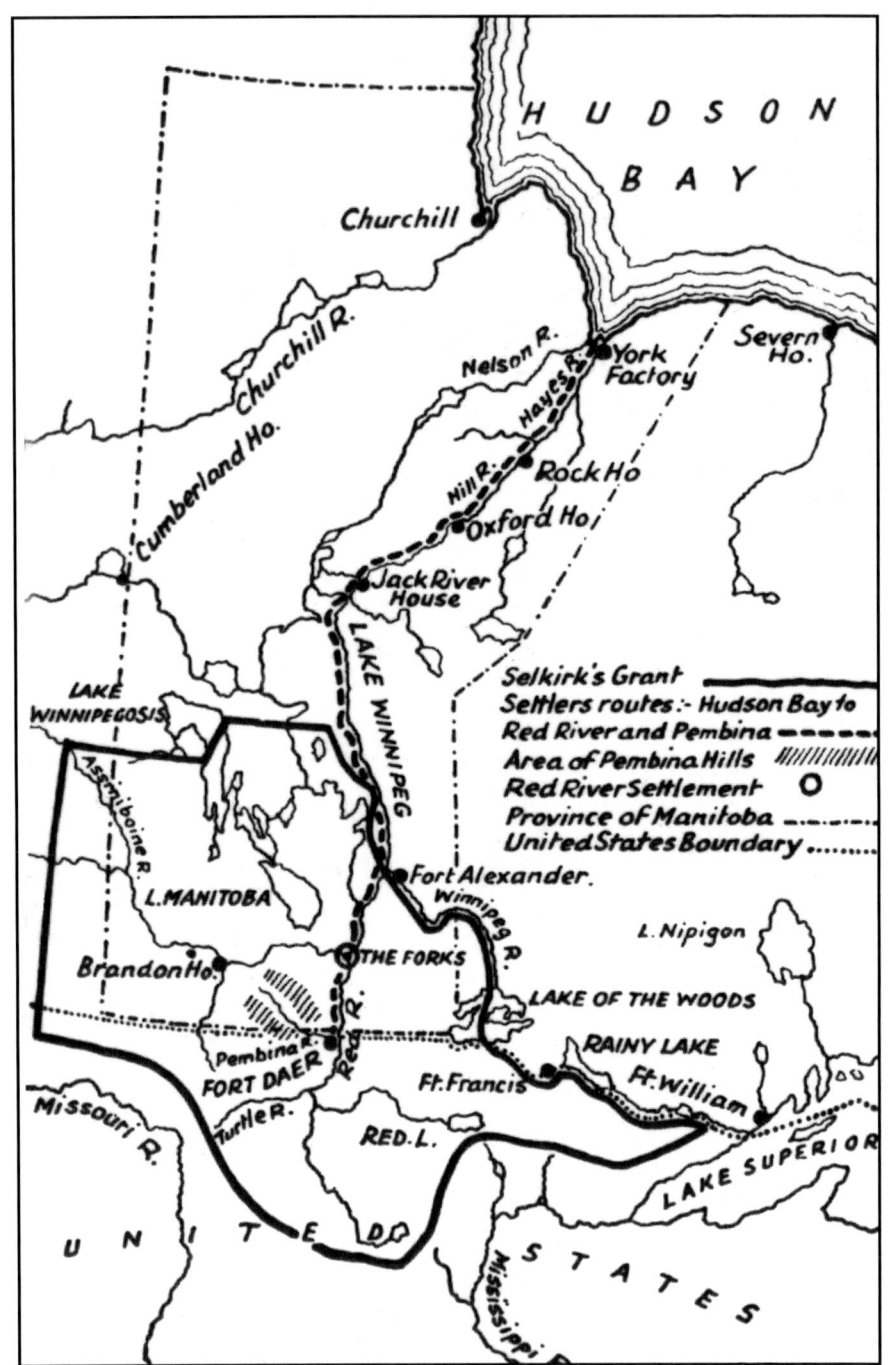

Grant to Lord Selkirk and the route travelled by early settlers from Hudson's Bay to Red River
GEORGE BLACK, MCGILL-QUEENS UNIVERSITY PRESS

Thomas and Barbara

and the NWC's many experienced men, he released the less-experienced employees, newer arrivals and many worn-out older servants. At the time of the merger in 1821 there were 1,983 Company employees. By 1825 only 827 remained and wages had been reduced considerably.[5]

If Thomas Wishart worked for the HBC, at all, it was only for a short time. He found a position in 1820 with the administrators of the Selkirk Colony, and in the same year he married Barbara Spence, the daughter of James Spence Jr. and his Native wife, Mary.

It was a turbulent time in the colony. The year before Wishart's arrival there had been a plague of grasshoppers. Crops, gardens, leaves—anything and everything green was eaten. In 1819, countless swarms emerged from the ground where larva had been deposited. Crops vanished as soon as the first sprouts appeared. The water became poisoned with swarms of the creatures. The settlers looked heavenward and wept.[6] A shortage of both food and seed, and an epidemic of measles and whooping cough added to the misery of the colony. Discontent with the conditions led to acts of lawlessness. It was not the best of times.

While Wishart is listed as a Colonial Servant from 1820 to 1824, there is no record of the capacity in which he served. He may have been employed in colony work: house building, road making or tripping (assisting with river travel).[7] Being an Orkney man like William Flett, he would have had schooling as a youth and would be able to read and write. Thomas' education would have been a valuable asset to the new colony during its desperate times.

With Simpson's restructuring of the Hudson's Bay Company, many retired traders and their families began to swell the colony. By 1822 there were 126 houses and 160 garden plots in the settlement.[8] Among the new settlers was Robert Logan who was married to a Native woman. He was to become one of the chief men of the Settlement, serving as a Councilor of Assiniboia from 1825–39.[9] HBC records indicate that Wishart served with Robert Logan in 1828, but we do not know how long his service lasted, nor in what capacity he served.

What Lies Behind the Picture?

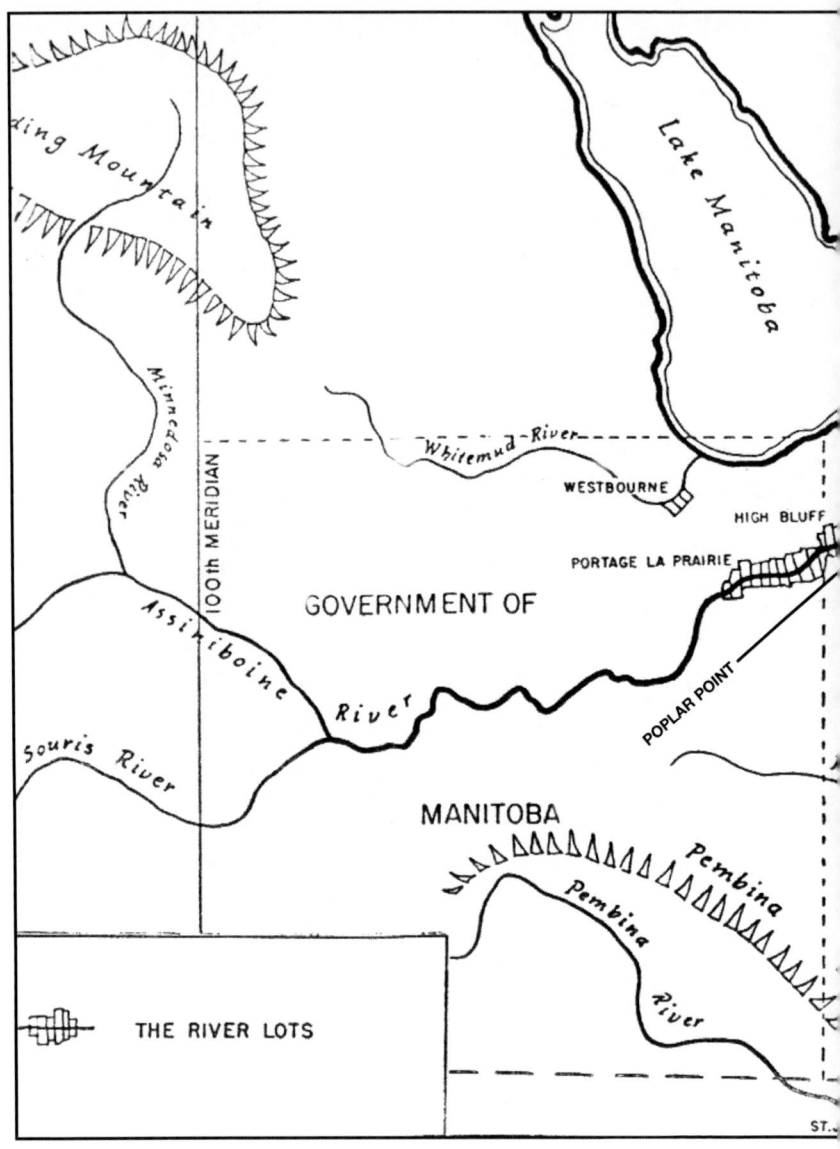

The Settlements
MANITOBA: A HISTORY, UNIVERSITY OF TORONTO PRESS

We do know that Thomas Wishart acquired land, Lot 29, along the banks of the Assiniboine in St. James Parish. By 1835 he and Barbara had five children and 11 acres under cultivation. They owned seven cattle and a Red River Cart.[10] Among the cattle were oxen used for pulling the plow and the cart. Their hold-

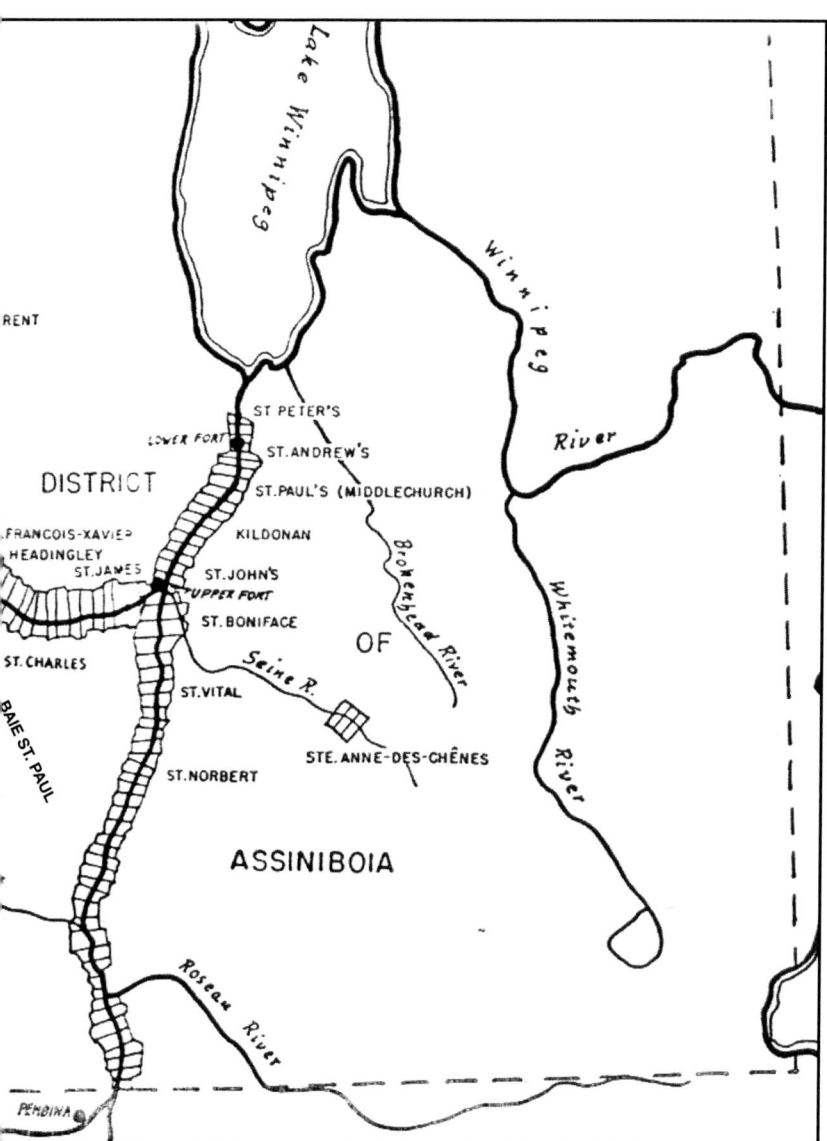

ings, while appearing modest, were about average in comparison with their neighbours.

Thomas, an Orcadian, and his Mixed-blood wife Barbara, were to have seven children. The fourth child was James Wishart, our great-grandfather, the man caught in the Great Blizzard of 1887.

What Lies Behind the Picture?

By the time James was born in 1830, Thomas and Barbara were beginning to farm the tiny plots on the banks of the Red River. By necessity, they engaged in three occupations in order to survive: farming, hunting and fishing.

The Red River Valley had attractions and disadvantages. The soil was rich and fertile. There were not many trees, so the expense and the labour of clearing the land was avoided. The heat in the summer could be oppressive, ranging from 35 to 40 degrees Celcius. Mosquitoes thrived, rising in clouds at every step if you deviated from the path or road, and horse and black flies tormented the settlers. In the winter biting winds, deep snow and intense cold reaching minus 45 degrees created a bleak landscape. Wolves stalked the livestock. One great drawback—more unpredictable than the vagaries of weather, mosquitoes and other insect pests—was the location on a flood plain. Serious flooding became one of the natural hazards of living in the settlement.

In the spring of 1826, Thomas and Barbara experienced the first of the settlement's great Red River floods. About 2:00 P.M. on May 5, the ice gave away "with an awful rush, carrying away cattle, houses, trees and everything else that came in its way."[11] The river reached a height of over 11 metres, forming a vast lake. No subsequent flood ever reached this height, not even the disastrous Red River flood of 1997, which covered 1,600 square kilometres.[12]

Confronted with a terrifying wall of water, Thomas and Barbara, along with other colonists, fled with their children, and what they could save of their belongings and flocks, to higher ground, possibly to Stone Mountain, a high ridge 18 metres above the prairie. Those who were unable to escape were rescued from watery graves by HBC men in their boats. Settlers watched their houses and possessions disappear or float upon the broad floodwaters.

When the flood drained away, the colonists returned to their river lots and again took up the toil of farming and the chase of the buffalo. Many in the colony, however, had borne all they could of the hazardous life and journeyed south to the Mississippi Valley in the United States. This emigration was

Thomas and Barbara

offset by a steady stream of retired fur traders, mainly Scots or Orcadians with their Native or Mixed-blood wives, whose dark-eyed children filled the schools of the settlement.[13]

Despite the locusts, fall frosts, mice, grubs and other afflictions, the plots lengthened their black strips along the riverbanks. As the number of steel ploughs increased, agriculture began to become more firmly established and soon a line of well-built houses lined the river lots. The population numbered about 5,000 by 1835. Still, the colony was dependent on the buffalo hunt for its main supply of food. Even when the crops became more abundant, "plains provisions" remained a large part of the Red River diet. Historian W. L. Morton makes this pertinent observation: "The long years of trial had ended in a compromise between the hunt and the plough, between dependence on the summer drift of the buffalo herds and the rhythm of seedtime and harvest."[14]

With the money he saved from his work in the Selkirk Colony, as well as the money earned as a ploughman-farmer in the Red River Settlement, Thomas had acquired by the late 1830s a house, barn and stable, one horse, four cows, one ox, two calves, a cart, harrow, canoe and 11 acres of land.[15]

Was it the continuing struggle to survive or was it their spirit of adventure that made Thomas and Barbara decide to pull up stakes? Thomas's decision to leave home and country to come to Rupert's Land was evidence of a boldness of spirit, but how about Barbara? Was she a reluctant or a willing companion?

Barbara's father, James Spence Jr., had been engaged by Captain John Franklin's second overland expedition to the Arctic in the years 1825–27. Spence was likely hired because of his experience and skills as a hunter, a runner who carried messages, and an interpreter. Before returning to the Red River Settlement, he sailed to England on the *Prince of Wales* with the expedition party in the fall of 1827.[16]

Barbara must have listened with great interest as her father recounted to the family his adventures with the Franklin's Expedition and his time in England. Perhaps Barbara, like her husband, embraced adventure.

What Lies Behind the Picture?

About 1837 or 1838, after the birth of their youngest child Elijah, Thomas and Barbara decided to strike out in search of a new home. Leaving two of the younger children, James, age seven, and Mary, age three, in the care of their maternal grandparents, the couple took the three older children, ranging in age from 10 to 15, and baby Elijah, and headed south in a party of other settlers. Their destination was Iowa, reported to be a fertile farming country. They settled in Clayton County.[17] Thomas and Barbara did not see two of their children, James and Mary, again.

JAMES AND ELIZA

CHAPTER 10

Eliza's Medicine Bag

IN WHICH WE COME TO THE COUPLE WHO INSPIRED US TO MAKE THIS JOURNEY TO OUR ROOTS: WHERE THEY MET; THEIR EARLY FORMATION; THE MARRIAGE OF A GIANT OF A MAN AND A PETITE WOMAN STEEPED IN NATIVE MEDICINE; AND THEIR MANNER OF LIFE.

At the age of seven, James Wishart watched his parents, Thomas and Barbara, leave for the United States. Why did the family leave him and his sister Mary behind? Perhaps it was felt they were too young to travel. I wonder about the pain a small brother and sister felt as they waved to their departing parents and siblings. Did they feel deep down they were never to see their parents again?

The two children were embraced as family by Barbara's parents, James Spence Jr. and Mary, a Native or Mixed-blood,[1] in the Red River Settlement or possibly nearby in the Indian Settlement. As James grew older he learned from his grandfather a variety of skills: hunting buffalo, stonemasonry, how to handle an axe in the construction of houses, river and cart freighting, as well as farming.

The Red River Settlement did not have a huge number of people living in it so most folk knew each other, if not well, at least casually. Although Eliza Flett was five years younger than James it is probable that they were acquainted with each other and attended the same school. They were married in September,

Eliza's Medicine Bag

Eliza Wishart
JAMES AND ELIZA'S BIBLE

1853, in St. John's Anglican Church. She was 18 and he was 23. They must have been a striking couple. Eliza was a graceful woman, small, not more than five feet, slender, relatively fair of face with delicate features. Her hair was black and straight, her lips thin, her mouth firm. James was a handsome, soft-spoken, giant of a man—six feet, six inches tall, with broad shoulders and muscular frame. His dark hair and beard framed a wide forehead, angular nose and firm jaw. Grandchildren of James and Eliza recall that as children they met their Grandpa

What Lies Behind the Picture?

James for the first time when he came to visit them after Grandma Eliza had passed away. "When he stood up he filled the doorway. As he was leaving he stood in their kitchen wearing his buffalo robe, coat and hat. He seemed to be a mountain of a man."[2]

James and Eliza were well aware of their Native ancestors and their way of maintaining a livelihood. They grew up in homes where floors were covered with mats woven with rushes. Meat was preserved by drying rather than salting. Raspberries, saskatoons, and blueberries were also preserved by drying. Eliza learned how to use the country's natural resources such as the wild potato and wild turnip, which sustained settlers in times of scarcity; the red willow whose inner bark, *kini-kinik,* was dried and rubbed and used as a substitute for tobacco, as well as for a poultice to treat infection and swelling; the inner bark of the poplar, which was eaten in the spring as a tonic; the buffalo root, which children chewed as treats; and the drink made from the sap of the white spruce as a remedy for scurvy. Eliza also learned various ways of cooking pemmican. One form was *rubaboo* which was made by boiling pemmican with potatoes, onions and other vegetables. Another was *rowshow*, made by mixing shredded pemmican with flour and water and then frying the mixture in a pan.[3] She also learned how to use other herbs, roots and bark for healing wounds and cuts, a knowledge which one day would save James' life.

Eliza was the daughter of Euphemia Halcro and Peter Flett, the youngest child of William Flett and Saskatchewan. Peter married Euphemia Halcro in 1834. The Manitoba Census of 1870 describes Peter and Euphemia as English half-breeds, Protestant, born in the North West and living at St. Paul (Parish) in the Red River Settlement. Peter and Euphemia had 15 children, nine of whom survived. Eliza (Elizabeth Amy), born on November 1, 1835, was the eldest.

Our first introduction to Eliza's Native heritage was in John J.

Eliza's Medicine Bag

Martin's account in *The Rosebud Trail*. In Martin's story, we learned that James Wishart, Eliza's husband, was caught in the Great Blizzard of 1887 and suffered from severe frostbite. Eliza saved James' life by "her knowledge of Indian medicine and surgery." This revelation sent us searching for our Native roots and in the process expanding our family tree. The discovery of relatives in Montana led not only to a reunion but also to a trunk which contained among other valuable keepsakes—Eliza's medicine bag.

In the task of linking together our ancestral chain, we did not stop and ponder the significance of Eliza's medicine bag, which tragically, along with other items in the trunk, was destroyed in a fire. We assumed that she, like many women of Native background, used roots, herbs and plants for medicinal purposes. This was our first conclusion; but another entry in Martin's book suggests that there was more to Eliza's knowledge of Native medicine. He writes:

In 1898, I had a sore on the palm of my hand which would not heal, someone told me to go to Mrs. Wishart. In the Wishart kitchen Eliza studied the wound awhile, then with difficulty (she was not strong and seemed quite lame) she got the "medicine bag." It was full of roots and hung high up on a spruce log knot. After selecting the right root she chewed it to a pulp, and placed it directly on the wound and wrapped it with buckskin. I do not remember how many treatments I had but my hand healed, and Herb [James and Eliza's youngest son] *remarked, "It was not the roots; it was mother's magic touch and her saliva that did the healing." She had inherited the magic of a medicine man from her ancestors.*[4]

Donna Sutherland, a historian specializing in fur trade family history and Native people, makes this observation:

Eliza's medicine bag is significant and tells us that she was a strong spiritual person and one who was highly respected. . . . Most often parents "knew" when a child showed special powers such as healing. When Eliza reached the appropriate age she would be encouraged to fast and dream to see if she did indeed have the powers that her parents believed she had. Once she took that initial step she would be encouraged

What Lies Behind the Picture?

to pursue her gift and would be taught by the Elders . . . about the medicinal properties of plants, roots, and herbs. . . . Eliza did not just pick up a medicine bundle one day and say "I think I'll try this." She learned that craft early and practiced it always.[5]

We do not know the personal details but it is probable that Eliza was deeply influenced, as a child and young woman, by Native culture—a culture in which spirituality permeates all of life—where the whole of life is experienced as an interaction with a creation which is alive with supernatural meaning.[6] Eliza's gifts of healing would have had a spiritual dimension.

From the time Eliza was very young, she experienced the influence of Christian missionaries in the Red River Settlement. They came with the underlying assumption that their task was not only to convert, but to begin the movement from the "savage" to the "civilized" and from an "inferior" culture to a "superior." Native spirituality was seen as inferior and pagan in its practices.

John Webster Grant, church historian, writes that there was general agreement by the European settlers that:

. . . a lower culture coming into contact with a higher one was doomed to extinction. Aborigines could hope to survive only by becoming like Europeans, and it was the responsibility of missionaries and administrators to give them all possible help.[7]

We may wince today at the near-absolute identification of Christianity with European culture but in that day it was largely unchallenged.

Among the early missionaries was the Rev. William Cockran who arrived in the Red River Settlement in 1825. He was sent by the Church Missionary Society (Anglican) of England. Hardworking and devoted, he typified the general European attitude toward the Native people. Their spirituality and morals were judged by British standards. In his reports to his superiors he made it clear that

. . . the Dominant race of this continent are the English and that the Indian and Half-breed would always be immoral,

Eliza's Medicine Bag

Missionary visiting Indians at Red River
S. DUFFIN, INDIAN COLLECTION, ARCHIVES OF MANITOBA

capricious, intractable, indolent, callous, prideful, wayward, extravagant, ingracious, improvident and careless.[8]

Cockran felt his work among the Native people would not succeed until they lived in one place, in a permanent settlement. Not only would it help him in his efforts to evangelize, it would provide an opportunity to teach farming and establish a school and a church. With the permission of the HBC, and the support of Peguis, the Saulteaux chief whom he befriended, Cockran established a permanent Native settlement on the banks of the Red River called St. Peter, or the Indian Settlement. The church was called St. Peter Dynevor. The Settlement included Saulteaux, Swampy Cree and Mixed-blood. By 1835, when Eliza was born, 60 children attended the school.[9]

Growing up in this setting Eliza learned Native ways and healing practices at a time when they were regarded with suspicion and contempt by the missionaries. Her parents, Peter and Euphemia, must have given quiet encouragement, as did Saskatchewan, her *ohkoma* (grandmother), who may have believed it was necessary to pass on to her granddaughter Native spirituality with its sacred knowledge, prayers and practices.

Like her parents and her grandmother, Eliza was baptized and attended church. She and James remained Anglicans until

What Lies Behind the Picture?

1877 when they became Wesleyan Methodists. She did not give up her medicine bag. She did not say, "I do not need this now. I have Christ." Rather, she found a way of understanding and expressing her Native spirituality while seeing herself as a faithful Christian.

James and Eliza Wishart became part of what the white settlers would call the "Half-breed" population of Red River. Both were of mixed-blood and were seen as such according to HBC archives.[10] They lived among the Métis and Mixed-blood who were now predominant in the Red River Settlement. They located themselves initially at St. Paul's Parish (Middlechurch) with lots located on both sides of the Red River.[11]

In 1861, A.K. Isbister, who was a Mixed-blood, wrote to England:
. . . it is an interesting fact that the half-castes or mixed race not only outnumber all the other races in the colony put together, but engross nearly all the more important and intellectual offices—furnishing from their number the sheriff, medical officer, the postmaster, all the teachers but one, a fair proportion of the magistrates and one of the electors and proprietors of the only newspaper in the Hudson's Bay territories. The mixed-race, from the inter-marriage during many generations of the Company's officers and servants with the native Indians, have, in fact, increased to such a degree that they are at the moment the dominant class in the country.[12]

After the flood of 1861 and with the influx of free traders and land seekers, James and Eliza and family moved to the growing settlement at Poplar Point and High Bluff. Government records in 1877 show that they lived in Poplar Point Parish, River Lot 48,[13] located between Poplar Point and High Bluff, Manitoba. The lot was a narrow strip, ten and a half chains in width and three kilometres long on both sides of the Assiniboine. (A surveyor's chain is 66 feet long, or about 20 m).

In addition to farming, James, like his Métis' neighbours, may have joined in the annual buffalo hunt, not only to replenish his family's larder, but to earn extra money by supplying fur traders with hides, and meat that could be preserved for pemmican.[14]

Eliza's Medicine Bag

Going to church in Rupert's Land
INDIAN COLLECTION, ARCHIVES OF MANITOBA

Supplying meat became an industry for both the Métis and the Mixed-blood families. As time passed the HBC needed more pemmican to feed labourers, as did the settlers who were travelling west in increasing numbers. As more settlers moved west, more buffalo had to be killed to meet the demands. The plains Natives depended on the buffalo for food, shelter and clothing; they became increasingly alarmed by the dramatic decrease in the herds. There were numerous conflicts between the Métis and the Natives, particularly with the Sioux who were further south and in whose territory the Métis often hunted.

> The word *Pemmican* derives from the Cree word for "he makes grease." This staple food was made by cutting buffalo meat into thin slices that were hung to dry in the sun on racks made of willows. When the meat was dry it was pounded into a fine powder, put into bags of buffalo hide, mixed with hot buffalo fat and cooled. It was then sewed up and sealed with tallow. The mixture was easily transportable, nourishing and filling, and could be kept for a long period of time without spoiling.

What Lies Behind the Picture?

James and Eliza, however, were primarily farmers. Despite countless setbacks agriculture finally took hold at Red River. Farming was bound to the river's edge as every lot was laid out with river frontage. The historian W. L. Morton describes the reason for the river layout:

> Water, shelter, ease of travel, drainage, the desire for neighborhood, the fixed belief that it was impossible to cultivate the plains, all these kept agriculture joined to the rivers. As a result, the lots in time were narrowly subdivided and settlement was scattered along the rivers as far south as the Pembina River, and as far west as Portage la Prairie before it extended a mile from the rivers.[15]

D ROUGHT WAS NOT UNCOMMON, AND THE DANGER OF FALL frost remained serious.

For James and Eliza, the farming year began in March with the sugar-making among the groves of ash-leaved maple, along the river loops of the Red and Assiniboine. The crop year began in late April or early May. When the land was dry enough, it was ploughed with iron or wooden ploughs. When the soil was ready, the wheat was broadcast by hand and then harrowed into the earth. Barley, oats and potatoes followed, with perhaps some dwarf Indian corn which was a favorite with those of Native blood.[16] If James joined in the buffalo hunt or freighting, Eliza, with the older members of the family, would carry on the daily chores. They would feed the animals and tend the garden.

As the wheat and barley ripened, the reaping began with sickles and scythes, cutting down with smooth, repeated strokes the stiff stalks of tawny wheat and golden barley. The women and children followed—raking, binding and stooking (setting up 8–12 sheaves of grain in a teepee-like formation to allow them to shed water and dry for harvesting). Threshing was done by flailing the ripe grain on the barn floor; then the grain was winnowed and sifted in the open air, and stored for grinding or for seed.

When potatoes had been dug up and stored and the stock

Eliza's Medicine Bag

driven home into the enclosures, James and the older boys turned their attention to the "mudding" of the house and the barn, and the cutting and hauling of wood for fuel and fencing. Cattle were butchered for home use, but more often for sale. James would rely on his hunting skills for killing deer and moose, which would provide meat for home consumption. As well, the meat from buffalo hunts that wasn't sold was dried and made into pemmican.

The buffalo hunt was not the only occupation of the Métis and the Mixed-blood of the Red River Settlement. The HBC had posts scattered from Lake Superior to the Pacific, from the Red River to the Yukon. This called for an extensive system of transport for the movement of trade goods and fur. The York boat had largely replaced the canoe as a bearer of cargo. In June, the brigades of four to eight boats put out from Lower Fort Garry and other HBC posts to make their long, perilous journeys down stream to York Factory. They returned in October as ice was freezing the backwaters.[17] As a farmer James was probably not involved in the boat brigades which consumed four months of the year, but cart freighting, which was seasonal, casual and varied, was likely another source of income for him and his family.

After 1850, when James was just 20, the carts were organized in brigades. They wound lurching and screeching to St. Paul, Minnesota, or overland to the West via Fort Carlton on the North Saskatchewan to Edmonton, which was the depot which supplied northern forts. The Red River remained the hub of the new transport system as it had been of the old.

CHAPTER 11

The Trek West and the Métis Struggle

HEREIN THE CONTEXT IS SET FOR THE STRUGGLE BY THE MÉTIS UNDER THE LEADERSHIP OF LOUIS RIEL TO MAINTAIN THEIR LAND RIGHTS AND IDENTITY, AND THE IMPACT THIS STRUGGLE HAS ON JAMES AND ELIZA.

SIGNIFICANT EVENTS WERE ABOUT TO CHANGE THE LIFE of the colony. The buffalo hunt had not disappeared when James and Eliza settled on the river, but its end was in sight. The steamboat would end the use of the York boat; and the railroad would eventually replace the winding cart brigades.[1] As the old order passed away, so did the buffalo hunt. In their time, Isaac Batt, James Spence Sr., William Flett Sr., Thomas Wishart and their Native and Mixed-blood wives saw buffalo herds like cloud shadows moving through the woods and meadows of the parkland out to the rolling prairies. With the disappearance of the magnificent buffalo herds by 1880 so went the life and livelihood, not only of the Native people, but also of many Métis; and so went the cart freighting by which many Mixed-blood made their living.[2]

Land and agricultural settlement began to assume greater importance. Native, Métis and Mixed-blood families had important rights to maintain in the lands of the Northwest. A land rush, or the threat of a land rush, created fear of dispossession. Any threat of removal from their roots and the loss of land rights

The Trek West and the Métis Struggle

provoked resistance. As it became more apparent that the new Government of Canada would not protect their land title, the people of Red River sought to protect themselves. They set up a provisional government of their own.[3]

The fundamental question was about authority. Who would control the new territory at the time of transfer of ownership from the Hudson's Bay Company to the Government of Canada? Was it to be the indigenous people of the Northwest, or the Canadian Party and the new immigrants who were anxious that the Red River become part of Canada?[4] Rumours spread that the newcomers had boasted that the half-breeds would soon be driven from the country, or kept as cart-drivers to bring in the vehicles of the new immigrants. Apprehension grew. The coming of strangers "was like the march of the sun, it could not be stopped."[5]

In 1868 the Imperial Parliament passed the Rupert's Land Act, preparing the way for the Canadian government to purchase Rupert's Land from the HBC. This set the stage for the Deed of Surrender. It was decreed on July 15, 1870, that Rupert's Land and the North-Western Territory would be admitted into Canada as the North-West Territories. Thus the transfer of land was completed along with the extension of Canadian law. The Canadian government saw the annexation as a simple matter of ending the title of the HBC in Rupert's Land and assuming for itself the area extending from Labrador to the Rockies, a territory as large as Europe. Historian W. L. Morton comments, "One of the greatest transfers of territory and sovereignty in history was conducted as a mere transaction in real estate."[6] Canada made no effort to give

> The Canadian Party leader was John Christian Schultz. From 1860 to 1869 this party worked and waited for the advance of Canada into the North West. They established contact with Canada First, a group in Ottawa and Toronto who believed in Canadian westward expansion, and in the innate superiority of white Anglo-Saxon Protestants.

What Lies Behind the Picture?

assurance to the indigenous people that land titles would be guaranteed; that Indian entitlement would be replaced by treaty; or that self-government, in due course, would be freely granted.[7]

Suspicion grew that the Canadian government would not prevent an outright invasion of the land rights of Native, Métis and Mixed-blood. The question was particularly acute for both the Natives and the Métis. The fear was not so strong among the Mixed-blood, such as James and Eliza, and the white settlers. Among the French Métis, however, the fear of domination by English-speaking newcomers was acute. The Métis leadership decided to take a stand in order to talk terms while resistance was still possible. On October 11, 1869, a party of Métis led by Louis Riel stopped government surveyors.

A larger confrontation was inevitable. On December 8, 1869, Riel issued the Declaration of Rupert's Land, in which a Provisional Government was proclaimed. It declared that the establishment of Canadian authority would be opposed until there was the assurance of good government in Rupert's Land and the Northwest.[8]

Tragically, any attempts at negotiation by the government were side-lined by the execution of Thomas Scott, a strong Canadian nationalist who refused to recognize the provisional government and urged his companions to do likewise. He was tried on two counts: insubordination and striking the guards. He was found guilty and condemned to be shot. In the face of pleas for mercy, Riel replied, "We must make Canada respect us."[9] On March 4, 1870, Scott was led out and shot before the walls of Fort Garry.

The execution of Scott proved to be not only a blunder, but unnecessary. Thomas Bumsted describes it as "a mistake which cost Riel and the Métis heavily."[10] Scott's death aroused tremendous hostility in the east, fanning the resentment of both the Canadian party and the Orangemen of Ontario. Because the provisional government had no legal credibility in the eyes of the Canadian government, Scott's killing was seen as a breach of the law of the land.

Were there tensions between the Métis of French background

The Trek West and the Métis Struggle

Louis Riel, 1844-1885
LIBRARY AND ARCHIVES OF CANADA

and the Mixed-blood of Orkney and English background when it came to supporting Riel's resistance? James and Eliza undoubtedly shared many of the Métis grievances. They wanted the river lots to be respected, as well as their title to the land. They also desired assistance with seed grain and implements, similar to what was being proposed in the Native treaties.[11] Like the Métis and the Natives, they would have resented not being consulted by the government. It is likely, however, that they were not convinced the strong action of the Métis in the resistance of 1869–70 was necessary or defensible.

What Lies Behind the Picture?

There was one other very important factor in their relationship to Riel and the unfolding of events. James and Eliza were Protestants. Prior to becoming Methodists, they had been Anglicans and were married in an Anglican Church. Further, James was an Orangeman, a society intended to uphold Protestantism and to oppose Catholic religion and influence. This would have put him at odds with the Roman Catholicism of his Métis neighbours,[12] although not all Orangemen were virulently anti-Catholic at the time. The couple moved easily amongst the Native people and the Métis, speaking Cree, Saulteaux (Ojibway) and French, but their political allegiances may have been another story. There is no doubt that James and Eliza had genuine grievances of their own. Nevertheless, they maintained a basic loyalty to the Crown and probably rejected the idea that the 1869–70 resistance was the answer to the grievances of the Natives, Mixed-blood and the Métis.

The militant element of the native population of the old Northwest, the Métis, through their resistance movement, did win a victory for their land rights, language and faith. This victory was consolidated in the Manitoba Act of 1870.[13] With the coming into being of the new province, however, government land grants promised to the Métis and Mixed-blood were slow in coming and badly administered. Many people built homes on land they had settled only to have their property taken from them and given to the white immigrants, who were rapidly moving into the new territory. Many Métis and Mixed-blood families despaired of ever settling their land grants, and they sold their paper claims or land scrips, as they were called, to the land speculators. Others never bothered to make a claim at all and moved west.

With the coming of Dominion land surveyors, part of James' land was taken from him. The surveyors changed the system of land plots that fronted on rivers to quarter sections of land, which did not need to be adjacent to rivers. It was only later determined that under the Manitoba Act James was an original Native settler and entitled to his land.[14]

There would be one last struggle by the Métis to establish

The Trek West and the Métis Struggle

themselves as a nation. Louis Riel would play a crucial part. James and Eliza were swept up in the struggle, their lives changed forever.

T HE DECISION TO ABANDON THE RED RIVER SETTLEMENT and move to unknown territory must have been difficult for James and Eliza. They had deep roots in the life and the land where they were born and raised. They had put considerable energy into farming, first at St. Paul's on the Red River and later at Poplar Point on the Assiniboine. They had established friendships in the colony and were active in the Wesleyan Methodist Church.[15]

They decided to leave because of their growing frustration with the government's continued foot-dragging on loans for seed and equipment. Even more disturbing, the Dominion land surveyors had appropriated land that James and Eliza believed rightly belonged to them. Many Mixed-blood and Métis neighbours, in their desperation with government policy, had already left for the United States or the North West Territories. Those who had not already left were a disheartened lot. Eastern settlers had little sympathy for those of mixed blood, even people like James and Eliza who had remained loyal to the Crown during the 1869–70 Resistance. Many newcomers considered the land rights of Natives and Red River inhabitants as a hindrance to settlement by the "right sort" of people.

Where would James and Eliza go? Many of the Métis who had left Manitoba had settled along the South Saskatchewan River, but the concern for land rights which the Métis had in Manitoba were being raised again in the District of Saskatchewan. Rumours in the Red River Settlement suggested that Riel had

---

By this time the North West Territories by Order-in-Council in 1882 had been divided into four districts: Alberta, Assiniboia, Saskatchewan and Athabasca.

What Lies Behind the Picture?

returned from the United States, to which he had fled, and had been welcomed with open arms in Prince Albert by Métis and English alike. James and Eliza, while agreeing with the Métis land claims, knew from experience that in another showdown with the Federal government, Riel would be the leader and Gabriel Dumont would be his lieutenant. The response of the Native people could only be guessed.

A family friendship helped them decide on their destination. Their good friends, Rod and Ben McKenzie, had gone west to a place called Red Deer Crossing, where they had set up a sawmill.[16] As the railroad had reached as far as the Rocky Mountains in 1883, they could board the train as it passed through the Settlement and enroute west to Fort Calgary. What farm equipment and livestock they couldn't take with them on the train, they would leave with their older children or sell. The most difficult part in their departure would be the children and grandchildren they would leave behind.[17] We can well imagine, as they faced the uncompromising reality of their situation, Eliza or James saying, "It will be sad to leave the older children behind, but with the arrival of the eastern settlers our homeland is now something quite different."

And there was their age, James was 55 and Eliza, 50. Perhaps it was Eliza who expressed hesitation, "James, we are not young anymore, we are in our fifties."

James would be reassuring, "We have our health, and the children still with us are young and strong." There was the question as to when to go. Why leave in the dead of winter? They undoubtedly discussed this many times and came to the conclusion that they needed to reach Red Deer Crossing in time to get settled before spring so they would be ready to work the land.

It must have been a tearful departure as James and Eliza left their home and their older children behind. They were consoled by the hope that they would finally find a place where they could be secure and make a living.

In mid-January of 1885, a train made its way westward. James and Eliza Wishart, and their five youngest children—Margaret (Jenny), David, Mary, Benjamin, and Herbert—whose ages

The Trek West and the Métis Struggle

Red Deer River Crossing
RED DEER AND DISTRICT MUSEUM AND ARCHIVES

ranged from 22 to 6, were among its passengers. While the rest of the family travelled in coaches, James and David huddled in a boxcar with their livestock. At night they kept warm under buffalo robes. During the day the heat from the animals' bodies, along with a fire in a small stove, staved off the bitter cold. As the train made its way kilometre upon kilometre through the wintry landscape, the family lived on a diet of pemmican, bannock, potatoes and preserves, which Eliza and the girls had prepared before their departure.

E. L. Meeres, author of *Homesteads that Nurtured a City (Red Deer)*, referring to contemporary accounts in the *Calgary Herald*, describes James and Eliza's journey to Red Deer Crossing.

> *Mr. Wishart and family from Manitoba are expected here this week. He is bringing in livestock and implements and intends to farm extensively in the spring. The stock will suffer from exposure, as this is not the season generally chosen for emigrating. Rumour hath it that two young ladies are with the party, and the weather worn bachelors are brightening up considerably. There is a splendid opportunity for an enterprising matrimonial agent in this quasi angel-foresaken region.*[18]

What Lies Behind the Picture?

Late in January of 1885, Jim, Eliza and family unloaded their belongings and livestock at "Number 12 Siding," later to become Gleichen, east of Calgary. Why they did not proceed by rail to Calgary is unknown. They may have thought the steel ended at Siding 12, but more likely they had learned from their friends, the McKenzies, that there was a well-worn Native and buffalo trail, known as the Rosebud Trail, which angled northward toward their destination. They began the 160 kilometre trek to Red Deer Crossing. They transported their household effects and farming equipment in horse-drawn wagons. While the women drove, the men followed on horseback, herding the livestock. Meeres writes, "When the mail driver passed them 22 miles north of Calgary at Brushy Ridge, the snow was deep and a heavy wind was blowing. It was 15 miles from the first house and 30 miles to where timber afforded any shelter."[19] At the end of the day's journey, which sometimes covered less than eight kilometres, the men cleared the snow away, pitched a tent and fed the livestock. The women made a fire, prepared a meal of bannock or a light flapjack. With the addition of sow belly and tea this made a sufficient meal. At night a single candle lit the interior of the tent. While Eliza and James lingered awake to talk of the day's experiences and what lay ahead, the rest of the family found vacant spots on the buffalo robes laid on the ground. Wrapping themselves in Hudson Bay blankets and more robes the weary travellers slept.

THE WISHARTS ARRIVED AT RED DEER CROSSING WITH their lives and their livestock intact.[20] They were warmly welcomed by the McKenzies whose home was adequate in size to include the exhausted Wisharts. Even in winter, the area looked promising for a homestead. Surely now their hope of a life free from discrimination and government interference might be realized.

My sister Shirley captures in a poem the trip west and the deep feelings aroused in Eliza as they left their homeland for Red Deer Crossing:

The Trek West and the Métis Struggle

ELIZA'S LAMENT

Bound to a land we must leave
Bound for a land we know nothing of
Bound by train for the Territories
Bound to my man and children
I must follow

Cold the winter
This one of 1885
Cold the morning we board the train
Snow cold as ashes of last night's stove
We leave nothing behind that cannot be carried
Or can walk onto the train
Horses cattle sheep carts wagons
Machinery furniture what food there is
Bound for a land we know nothing of

Long the days
Long the nights
Children and animals restless
Slowly the train moves
Through a land of stark white
Mile after mile
We are bound for the territories
Bound to my man and children
I must follow

Our eyes follow the track
The endless track
There is no end and no beginning
My man and I are past our middle years
What way of life awaits us
Bound for a land we know nothing of?

The first part of the journey ends
The train grinds
Screams to a stop
We unload the horses cattle sheep
Carts wagons furniture what food remains

What Lies Behind the Picture?

Here by a place
They call Siding Number 12

We hitch the cattle and sheep behind
We load the furniture
All our wordly goods
We bind these tight with ropes

We are almost there
Our friends have come ahead to meet us
Shelter for the animals
Shelter for us
We will begin to build
We will bind our lives together

Bound to a land we had to leave
Bound to a land we know nothing of
Bound to my man and children
I have followed.[21]

In February, a few days after James and Eliza's arrival at Red Deer Crossing, Louis Riel called a meeting of the Métis in Batoche. The petition that had been sent to Ottawa by Riel on behalf of the Métis concerning their grievances was met with the usual foot-dragging. They waited patiently for a reply. Finally, on February 2, 1885, a member of the Territorial Council wired Ottawa to say the Métis were showing "great discontent at no reply to representation." On February 4, Prime Minister John A. Macdonald wired the Lieutenant-Governor of the North West Territories, Edgar Dewdney, saying that the cabinet had decided to "investigate the claims of the half-breeds."[22]

When the government finally responded in a concrete way, it was too late. On March 19, Riel made the decision to elect a provisional government just as he had done prior to the founding of Manitoba.[23] This time, however, there was an important difference: the country over which he now proposed to set up a government was indisputably part of the Dominion of Canada; it was not stateless as Rupert's Land had been in 1869. The troubles began again.

CHAPTER 12

Prairie Fires

Wherein the serenity and promise of a new life for James and Eliza at Red Deer Crossing is interrupted by events at Duck Lake, Battleford and Frog Lake, signaling the beginning of the North-West Rebellion and leaving James and Eliza pondering their vulnerability.

The spring of 1885 came early at Red Deer Crossing. By March, James and Eliza were likely comfortably settled in their new home. James and their son David built their log house in a clearing sheltered by spruce and aspen on the lip of a hill overlooking two small lakes. The family had been attracted by the wild loveliness of the spot, its tree-clad hills, its lakes, and the fertility of the rich black soil. James and David were skilled axe men, and in their spare time perhaps they helped build log houses for other settlers who were moving into the area. Among the settlers were the Lennies. They had set up a "stopping house" for travellers across from the trading post. Tom Lennie was an Englishman. His wife, Mary, like James and Eliza, was a Mixed-blood from Manitoba who had experienced the first uprising.[1] Like the Wisharts, the Lennies had come to stake out a new life for themselves.

The Crossing was taking on a life of its own. Shortly after the railroad reached Fort Calgary in 1883, a four-horse stagecoach route to carry mail and passengers had been established between Fort Calgary and Fort Edmonton. It left Calgary on

What Lies Behind the Picture?

Monday and arrived in Edmonton on Friday, returning the following week. If nothing interfered, the mail reached the Crossing from Calgary every two weeks. A small trading post and post office had been built a little back from the Red Deer River. James and Eliza anxiously awaited mail and news from their family in Manitoba.

They did not lack for the basic necessities of life, since they could buy supplies at the trading post. There was an abundance of game. Although the buffalo had disappeared, there was meat from deer, moose, geese, sharp-tailed grouse, ruffed grouse and a dozen different kinds of ducks. Fish were plentiful in the nearby lakes, streams and rivers. As the season progressed, there was the promise of wild fruit: strawberries, raspberries, saskatoons, chokecherries, currants, gooseberries and cranberries, which were preserved by drying in the sun. The berries would add relish to their winter food. It was truly a land of plenty.[2]

Dave trapped muskrats on the lakes below their home and sold them at the post for five cents a pelt. Jenny and Mary gathered mud hen eggs when eggs became scarce for cooking.[3] Life had all the appearance of tranquility.

With the advent of spring settlers began planting their crops. News of Riel's return to the North West may have made James apprehensive. During the first uprising in Manitoba, he had seen the tremendous hold Riel had on the people.

The Riel who answered the call of his people in 1884 was fundamentally different from the successful leader of the 1869–70 Red River Resistance. He now regarded himself as God's personal emissary and the Métis as God's chosen people,[4] whose mission was to create a homeland in the North West for the Natives, and other oppressed people in preparation for the day of judgment.[5] Riel was also attempting to recreate in the North West wilderness a consecrated state for the militant propagation of the Catholic faith. His council had gone so far as to proclaim the establishment of "The Living Catholic Apostolic and Vital Church of the New World" and had designated Archbishop Bourget of Montreal as its Pope. Louis Riel was proclaimed a prophet. At his suggestion, the days of the week were renamed so that each might have some religious significance. Saturday was chosen as the Sabbath.[6]

James had every reason to believe the prairie rebellion would spread further west. Already Riel was sending appeals to the Natives and Métis, "Justice commands us to take up arms." On the Saskatchewan side of present day Alberta, Fort Pitt and Battleford were targeted. Riel wrote to the Métis:

Be ready for everything. Take the Indians with you. Gather them from every side. Take all the ammunition you can, whatever storehouses it may be in. Murmur, growl and threaten. Stir up the Indians. Render the Police of Fort Pitt and Battleford powerless. . . . Have confidence in Jesus Christ. Place yourselves under the protection of the Blessed Virgin.[7]

Battleford was 160 kilometres west of Batoche and a lesser distance from the present-day Alberta border, where 2000 Cree lived on reserves. Among them, the first to respond to the rapidly moving events were the Cree of Poundmaker's band.

Poundmaker, the son of an Assiniboine father and a Mixedblood mother, was in his mid-thirties, intelligent, dignified and eloquent. His adoption by Chief Crowfoot of the Blackfoot cemented ties between two powerful Native foes, the Cree and Blackfoot. He had reason to be dissatisfied with the federal Indian policy. The government had done little to assist the Cree in the first few years following the establishment of Treaty Six in 1876. This neglect combined with the loss of their major source of sustenance, the buffalo, and the failure of the government to help establish a strong agricultural base on the reserves meant severe hardship. In their book *Loyal to Death: Indians and the North West Rebellion,* historians Blair Stonechild and Bill Waiser underline the government's complicity in this state of affairs: [They] "reduced the Indian population on the prairies to a state of wretchedness that has no equal in modern Canadian history. For those chiefs and their followers who chose treaty, the Queen's hand was often empty, when not shaped in a fist."[8]

The North West Rebellion of 1885 began at Duck Lake, some 50 kilometres southwest of Prince Albert, in present day

What Lies Behind the Picture?

Saskatchewan. On March 26 a small party of North West Mounted Police rode toward Duck Lake for supplies. They turned back after being fired upon. Superintendent L. N. F. Crozier with 56 Mounties and 43 Prince Albert volunteers rode from Fort Carlton to Duck Lake to assert police authority. They were intercepted by Métis and Natives. Attempts at negotiation with their commander, Gabriel Dumont, failed when shots were fired. Crozier's forces retreated. Five of Dumont's men were killed, including his brother Isidore, and three, including Gabriel Dumont himself, were wounded. Crozier lost 12 men and 11 were wounded. Duck Lake gave Riel an important victory.[9]

Learning from messengers of the victory of Riel and his forces over Crozier and his force of Mounties and volunteers at Duck Lake, Poundmaker moved on Battleford.

On March 30, 1885, the Eagle Hill Cree were joined by some Assiniboine who had murdered their hated farm instructor, James Payne, and two other white men. The people of the village of Battleford and the settlers in the vicinity were warned of the approaching Natives and fled to the Mounted Police fort. Five hundred people, including three hundred women and children lived in terror in the small police fort. The desired interview with John Rae, the Indian agent, to address grievances failed. Despite Poundmaker's counsel of restraint, the Cree sacked the village, and for four weeks the fort was under a virtual state of siege. Every house and store, including the HBC post, was emptied and destroyed. When nothing remained inside, the houses were set on fire. The Cree then ranged beyond the town to farms, igniting everything in sight.[10]

On April 2, at Frog Lake, a small hamlet on a Native reserve in present-day eastern Alberta, a bloody massacre took place. Wandering Spirit, the war chief in Big Bear's band, and his followers, ignoring Big Bear's protests, killed nine people and burned the village. Among those who survived and were taken into captivity were Theresa Gowanlock and Theresa Delaney whose husbands had been killed.[11] The Frog Lake massacre and the captivity of the two white women inflamed passions in Ontario.

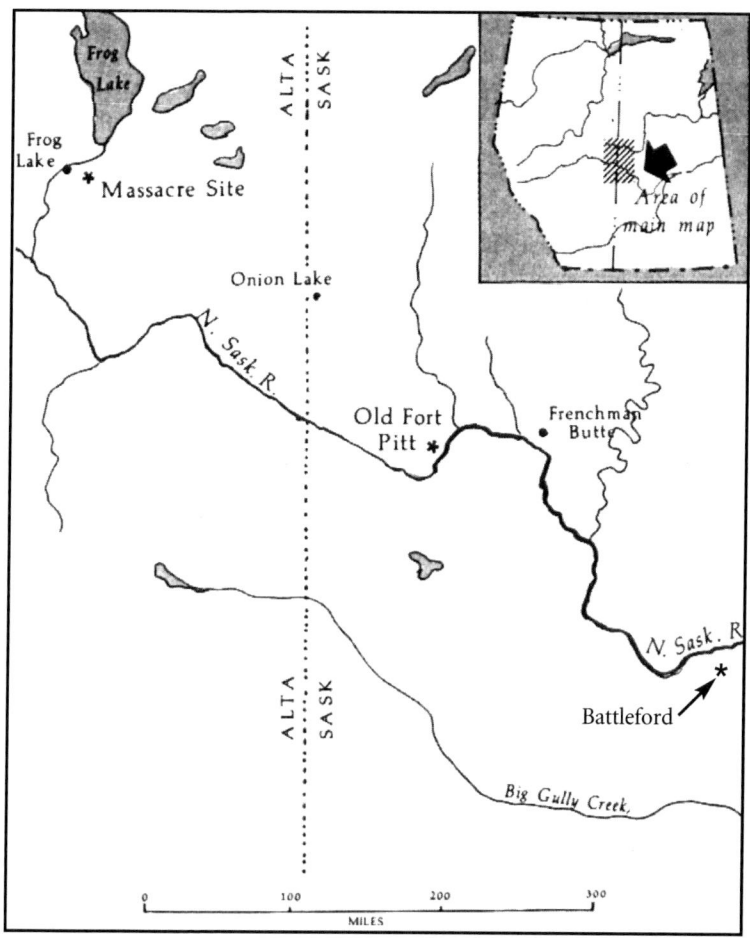

Saskatchewan River country
BEAL AND MACLEOD, *PRAIRIE FIRE*, HURTIG PUBLISHERS

The uprising, like a prairie fire out of control, was rapidly moving closer and closer to Red Deer Crossing.

JAMES MAY HAVE NOTICED BEFORE OTHERS AT RED DEER Crossing that the Natives in the area were anxious, possibly because of the news of events further north. Until then, the settlers in the district had been friendly to the local Native people, and this was reciprocated. The Cree often visited the home of James and Eliza as well as those of the white settlers and were polite and respectful. Now, however, increasing numbers began camping on the river flat north of the Crossing. James' apprehension grew as the sound of singing, rifle fire and horses snorting and milling echoed from their camps. Within a few days, the Natives' attitude had changed from friendliness to open hostility.[12] They began their war chants and drumming.

The settlers, realizing that their situation was becoming tenuous, held a meeting to take stock. In number, they were a mere handful with few firearms. The Cree far outnumbered them. They decided, however, to wait a few days hoping the danger would pass.

On the afternoon of April 7, 1885, Annie Gaetz, who lived on a farm home near the Crossing, heard voices and shouting. Looking down the trail she saw a dozen Native men approaching on horseback. As they came closer, she was terrified to see that they were wearing war paint, chanting and haphazardly firing their guns in the air. She hurried the children into the woods behind the house, telling the older ones to go to the fields where the men were working. Riding into the yard, the men dismounted and without invitation simply walked into the Gaetz home and demanded food. Mrs. Gaetz hurriedly complied. Sitting at the table with their rifles, the visitors proceeded to eat their fill of cold meat, beans and bread. Rising, and without a word, they walked out and disappeared down the trail.[13]

Late on the same afternoon, Ray Gaetz, the trader, was boiling his kettle for some tea on a campfire outside the trading post. The sound of horses' hooves made him look up. A lone horseman leading an extra horse approached rapidly from the north. Hurriedly dismounting, he asked Ray to lend him his saddle horse. Gaetz protested until the rider told him that he was a government courier. He had been sent to warn settlers that the Natives in the north had broken out in rebellion and that all the settlers were to gather at Fort Calgary for protection.[14]

On hearing the news, Ray ran across the road to tell Tom and Mary Lennie. Mary, remembering what had happened to her and her family in the first Riel resistance, fainted from fright.[15] When she recovered, she and Tom hastily gathered

Prairie Fires

together their belongings and left for Calgary under cover of night. During the day they hid in coulees. Upon reaching Calgary, they made the decision to continue to Montana.[16]

James and Eliza probably felt reasonably secure in their relationships with the Native people. They were not at all sure, however, how the Natives would react if they decided to travel with the white settlers, or how they, as Mixed-blood, would be received in Calgary. Hostility toward Riel and any one of mixed-blood was now strong. It is highly likely that they decided to stay for the time being.

The arrival of the courier galvanized the settlers. They decided to leave the Crossing by daylight rather than slipping away during the night as the Lennies had done. About noon on April 8, 1885, the settlers gathered at the Crossing's trading post. Each family had hastily prepared provisions for the five-day trip. The Natives, who had also gathered at the Crossing, watched in sullen silence as the little caravan left. The settlers were sure that their homes would be looted and burned and their livestock rustled.[17]

As they made their way south they expected to get meals and more provisions at the several stopping houses between Calgary and Red Deer. This was not to be, as all the white settlers had fled to Calgary, leaving no one along the trail. Each night the Crossing settlers drew their wagons into a circle for protection and formed a corral to protect their horses from thieves. While the men took turns on sentry duty, the women and children slept in the wagons. One night shots were fired, and the camp went on the alert. It was later discovered that a group of Mixed-bloods had fired the shots in the hope of stampeding the horses.[18]

The trip to Calgary usually took five days, but the anxiety of the party meant that they made the trip in three days. On arrival in Calgary, the settlers pitched their tents near the fort along with other settlers and prepared to wait for news of further developments.

There was great uncertainty as to whether the Native people in the North West would support the rebels. They outnumbered the white population by two to one. Not the least of the settlers' fears were the 5000 Natives who made up the Blackfoot

What Lies Behind the Picture?

Confederacy.[19] Would they join the Cree to the north and fight alongside Riel?

On April 11, Father Lacombe met with representatives of the Blackfoot Confederacy at Gleichen. In exchange for the government's promise of protection and food, Chief Crowfoot reaffirmed his allegiance to the Crown and in a special telegram sent to the prime minister said the following: "Should any Indians come to us and ask us to join them in a war we will send them away. I have sent messengers to the Blood and Peigans . . . to tell them . . . what we intend to do about trouble . . . We will remain loyal to the Queen whatever happens."[20]

Nevertheless, among the white settlers there remained great anxiety often bordering on hysteria. The news of the Métis victory at Duck Lake and the Frog Lake massacre of nine people, including the taking of two white women as hostages by members of Big Bear's tribe, sent shock waves throughout the countryside. Farms and ranches were abandoned, and home guards were formed in the larger communities.

Two days after the Frog Lake massacre, the news reached Edmonton, which had more reason to be fearful than most centres in the North West. Strategically located, it was as a major trading centre, the most important HBC trading post between Battleford and the Rocky Mountains. It was, however, a long way from help in case of trouble. To add to the anxiety, the telegraph went dead.[21] The crown timber agent sent a letter to his superiors about the fear that gripped the town. He wrote, "We do not know the hour the Indians in our midst will rise, and if they do, God only knows the consequences . . . without outside assistance, [we] will be at the Indians' mercy."[22]

James Mowat, a courier, rode to Calgary for help. He carried a message from the local defense committee to General T. B. Strange, who was in charge of the defence forces in Alberta. It read, "Have wired Sir John. Indians on the war path. Send us men and arms immediately. Can't you help us at once?"[23]

As the courier rode for help, the townspeople began moving their families inside the HBC fort and strengthening the rather dilapidated stockade.[24] Little did they realize that the Native people on the surrounding reserves were equally upset by the news. The possible over-reaction of the white population heightened their anxiety.[25]

Fort Macleod also began preparing for an attack. A police escort was assigned to move the women and children from the fort to Calgary. A line of mounted couriers positioned every 20 kilometres was set up to relay messages between Fort Macleod and Calgary.

Fear became panic. Shortly after their arrival in Calgary, many settlers gathered on a Sunday night for a worship service. A latecomer joined the congregation. As a joke, while heads were bowed in prayer, he whispered, "The Blackfoot are marching on the town."[26] Within minutes, the news was circulated among the congregation and people began to leave. When the minister was finally informed as to why his congregation was dwindling so rapidly, he dismissed the rest and told them to go quietly to their homes. The women and children, however, were hastily taken into the fort. The men gathered what firearms they could muster. Those who had none took up picks, shovels and whatever came to hand. So armed, they went forth expecting to do battle.[27]

As they reached the Blackfoot encampment, which was quite close to Calgary, they discovered that all was quiet. The Natives were sleeping peacefully. It was only then that the armed contingent discovered that they had been misled by an idle rumour. As nerves frayed, events could easily have taken an ugly turn against a peaceful Native community.[28]

The settlers' anxiety was somewhat relieved when on April 16, 1885, the 350 strong 65th Mounted Royal Rifles from Montreal arrived in Calgary. These troops, along with the Alberta Mounted Rifles, the Winnipeg Light Infantry, Steele's Scouts and one muzzle-loading-nine-pounder field gun, constituted the fighting force in the region. Major General Strange was put in command of these forces, which were soon augmented by a detachment of North West Mounted Police.[29]

The Government had finally begun to respond to the crisis.

What Lies Behind the Picture?

Not only had it realized the potential danger to white settlers, if there was a general Native uprising, but also the possibility that the Natives would add additional forces to Riel's warriors.

Despite the unsettled conditions, several of the men from Red Deer Crossing, who were anxious about their homes and livestock, decided to return. Others waited until they could leave with the Canadian troops. Before leaving Calgary, the government supplied the settlers with arms and ammunition.[30] Accompanying the returning settlers were Father Lacombe and the Reverend John McDougall.

These were long and anxious days for James and Eliza and their family. No stage coach was running, and no traders and freighters were stopping at the Red Deer Crossing trading post. There was no news of the outside world except that which came by Métis riders and Native scouts. James and Eliza likely did what they could to keep watch over the deserted settlers' homes. When the settlers did return, they were surprised to find that the Natives had done no looting.[31] They rounded up livestock and work on the land resumed. Still, there was deep anxiety. James and Eliza, from their experience in Manitoba, were by now knowledgeable witnesses of Riel's ambitions for a state and his hold on the Métis. They were undoubtedly anxious that the worst was yet to unfold.

CHAPTER 13

The Aftermath of the Rebellion

WHEREIN IS DESCRIBED THE END OF THE NORTH-WEST REBELLION WHICH WAS TO HAVE DISASTROUS RESULTS FOR MÉTIS, NATIVE AND MIXED-BLOOD, LIKE JAMES AND ELIZA.

On the morning of Tuesday, May 12, the North-West Rebellion ended with the Battle of Batoche. Historians Bob Beal and Rod Macleod describe the conclusion in *Prairie Fire*: "It was the only clear-cut defeat the rebels suffered but it was enough. They scattered, never again to reassemble as an army."[1] At Batoche, a people who wanted recognition as citizens of the North West were forced to surrender. And so ended a rebellion that could have been avoided.

Gabriel Dumont, the brilliant Métis strategist, escaped to Montana. Riel allowed himself to be captured. He was tried for treason in Regina. As the weeks in prison wore on without a hopeful word in the struggle to save him, he began work on his *Dernière Mémoire*. In it he described the history of his people as well as their social and psychological struggle. He spoke of the

> Batoche, the Métis capital, located 44 kilometres southwest of Prince Albert in today's Saskatchewan, was a cluster of shacks, a church and a few large houses.

need for pride in being mixed-blood ("We are Métis"); and of their love for their wilderness land. He described the excitement of the hunt: "the coursers rearing, neighing, dancing, digging at the ground with eager hooves." He spoke of the way the Métis had helped the Native people to reconcile to the inevitable arrival of settlers; and he claimed that the Métis "at the price of their blood gave tranquility to the Northwest."[2]

Apart from this eloquent writing there is little record of his words during his last moments. Father André, the priest who accompanied him to the gallows, had trouble keeping his composure. It is reported that Riel looked at him and said, "Courage, mon père;" and as the hangman came forward and slipped the noose over his head he prayed in French "I believe still; I believe in God to the last moment . . ." On November 16, 1885, as Riel stood on the gallows platform, Father McWilliams led the last prayer, in English. Riel's voice was faint but clear:

Our Father, who art in heaven, hallowed be Thy name. Thy kingdom come. Thy will be done on earth as it is in heaven. Give us this day our daily bread, and forgive us our trespasses, as we forgive them that trespass against us. And lead us not into temptation, but deliver us . . .

Before he could finish, the trapdoor opened and his body plunged downward nine feet. Riel quivered as he swayed on the taut rope. A few minutes later, two doctors pronounced him dead.[3]

Long before Riel was tried, the immensity of ill will generated by the rebellion toward anyone of mixed-blood began to be evident. James and Eliza anticipated that it would lead to persecution, not only of the Métis, but all those of Mixed-blood families. They made the decision to head to Montana by way of Pine Lake, southeast of Red Deer Crossing.[4]

Their hunch was correct. Several disbanded regiments of Canadian militia, which had formed during the Rebellion, began to make unchecked raids across the prairies. Nicholas C. P. Vrooman in the Introduction to Joseph Kinsey Howard's *The Strange Empire,* writes:

The rogue militiamen received land warrants for their serv-

The Aftermath of the Rebellion

ice to the country during the rebellion. The land came from the Métis they uprooted. A virtual bounty situation existed: for every Métis killed or dispossessed and driven away, a parcel of land became available. . . . From 1885 Métis lived essentially as refugees.[5]

The Métis suffered widespread demoralization: loss of land, status, dispersal to marginal rural areas and the peripheries of Indian reserves.[6] To this day, they remain grievously hurt by the manner in which they were treated.

The Native population was not to fare much better. Few had taken part in the Rebellion. Treaty obligations had made them view themselves as full partners in the new legal order. With the Rebellion, however, hysteria among the white population became rampant, particularly following the events of Frog Lake. Despite the fact they were unharmed, false stories were circulated about the treatment of the two women taken in captivity.[7] In the words of historian Sarah Carter:

If there was a shred of tolerance before, or the possibility of working towards a progressive partnership, it was shattered in 1885, as thereafter Aboriginal people were viewed as a threat to the property and safety of white settlers.[8]

The rebellion was used by the government to falsify and magnify the threat of Native people. Following 1885, policies were implemented that attacked the tribal system and rigidly supervised and monitored the movements and activities of reserve people.[9] Hayter Reed, who rose from an Indian agent at Battleford to Deputy Superintendent General of Indian Affairs, described the Indians as "a foreign element" who constituted a source of danger. They had to be broken up, disbanded and assimilated. He was stating goals that were already accepted in the 1876 Indian Act but with 1885 were pursued with greater intensity.[10] Among those goals, boundaries between Native and White were to be rigidly maintained. A pass system was initiated which monitored where, how and when contact with white people could take place.[11] Reserves were robbed of any potential source of revenue. By the late 1880s, just as the Native people were demonstrating a capacity for success as farmers, white farmers

What Lies Behind the Picture?

in Manitoba and the North West Territories (present day Saskatchewan and Alberta) complained that Indian farmers were "unfair" competition, because of the government assistance offered in making the transition to farming. In response the government enacted the "peasant farm policy" in 1889. Reserve farmers were to reduce their acreage in favour of smaller farms of only a single acre, and their herds to a cow or two, "emulating peasants of other countries."[12] Sarah Carter writes: "Reed argued that labour-saving machinery might be necessary for other farmers, but Indians had to first experience farming with crude and simple implements. Otherwise they would be defying immutable laws of evolution, and would be making an unnatural leap."[13] This policy along with the "Pass and Permit" system which restricted Native people from leaving the reserve, or selling their produce on or off the reserve, meant that Native communities and individuals never benefited from the right of the open and the free trade afforded other farmers.[14] Reserve farmers were deprived of any potential source of revenue.[15] Government policies increased dramatically the political, economic and social distance between Natives and Whites. The result was a virtual wall between them.

A century and a quarter later, Native people are still engaged in the struggle to overcome racial profiling and to regain their rights to land and resources. In 1969 in his book *Unjust Society,* Harold Cardinal wrote: "We remain acutely aware of the threat—the loss of our Indian identity, our place as distinct, identifiable Canadians."[16] That threat remains today. While there are encouraging signs of progress, there remains the Indian Act. Thomas King in the Massey Lectures of 2003 described the Act as:

> *A magical piece of legislation that twists and slides through time, transforming itself and the lives of Native people at every turn. And sprinkled throughout the act, which, among other things, paternalistically defines who is an Indian and who is not, are amendments that can make an Indian disappear in a twinkle ... Hocus-pokus! Indians. Now you see them. Now you don't.*[17]

The Aftermath of the Rebellion

The year 1885 was an important turning point in Canadian history. Some historians, such as Thomas Bumsted, argue that it might be a more important watershed than 1867.[18] The transcontinental railroad, which was to hold the country together, was completed in 1885. In the same year, however, the young nation was divided by tensions which have characterized its life ever since. The tension, which arose between French- and English-speaking Canadians over Louis Riel, remains today. Likewise, the tension and distance between Native and non-Natives has remained an open wound. As always, the fate of the Mixed-blood is caught in between and submerged in the Native and the Métis struggle for rights.

CHAPTER 14

Journey to the Promised Land

In which James and Eliza anticipating animosity and persecution leave Red Deer Crossing and head for Montana only to find a place to call home beside the River of Many Rosebuds.

The year 1885 was also an important turning point in the lives of James and Eliza Wishart. After their arrival in January, it would seem they had become well respected among the settlers at Red Deer Crossing. Yet given the bad will generated toward the Métis and the Native people by the Rebellion, they knew that their situation would surely change as more settlers moved in. Anticipating animosity, they disposed of their land at Red Deer Crossing to John J. Gaetz. Leaving behind their initial hard work to prove up their homestead, they packed up their worldly goods, livestock and the family members who had accompanied them on their journey west—David, Mary, Benjamin and Herbert. They headed south by way of Pine Lake and the Rosebud Trail toward Montana. The trail they chose took them through Blackfoot country, tribes not involved in the uprising. By choosing this route, they hoped they would avoid any marauders recently released by the militia.

Not all the family left the Crossing. Jenny, the eldest daughter stayed behind. Among the 20 militiamen left at Fort Normandeau, which had been built near Red Deer Crossing in response to the

Journey to the Promised Land

Rebellion, she found a husband, Private Clarendon (Clarence) Wilson. Racial prejudice was not in his make-up and when he was demobilized, he and Jenny were married.

James and Eliza, however, decided to seek a new homeland. After several days' travel, the family came within sight of the Rosebud River, which the Blackfoot had given the name *Akokiniskway,* the "river of many rosebuds." The river wound its way through verdant valleys and grasslands. Deer and antelope grazed in the distance. A coyote was stalking unsuspecting mice. No human habitation was in sight. It was June. They camped.

As James and Eliza emerged from their tent the next morning, the sunlight shone down the valley upon thousands of budding wild rosebushes. James, over-whelmed with the sight, turned to Eliza who was building the campfire and said, "This is too good to leave, here is the promised land; we go no further."[1] By the river of many rosebuds they established their homestead in what became known as Redland, thus becoming the first settlers in the Rosebud area.

JAMES AND ELIZA LIVED THROUGH HISTORIC AND TROUBLING times, many of which were associated with one of the most controversial figures in Canadian history, Louis Riel. To some, Riel was a hero, a statesman and The Father of Manitoba. To others, he was a religious fanatic, a madman, a rebel.[2] For James and Eliza he was likely a mixture of all of these. Whatever his reputation, and legacy, his actions had a dramatic impact upon their lives.

James and Eliza had lived through the first act of resistance led by Riel in 1869. They were subjected to the discriminatory government policies in Manitoba following the Manitoba Act of 1870. In January 1885, seeking a new life they moved westward, overcoming the hazards of winter travel, to settle near Red Deer Crossing. They weathered the gathering storm as the North West Rebellion of 1885 reached from the District of Saskatchewan into what was to become Alberta. When it finally reached its climax at Batoche, they anticipated the fallout and, like wandering

What Lies Behind the Picture?

nomads, were on the move again. Through it all, they remained firm in their hope of finding a place to call home. As they faced the future, they bore the anxiety of being treated as outcasts. Never again could they hold up their heads with pride, for to speak of who they were and where they came from could put them in mortal jeopardy.[3]

James and Eliza did not go to Montana. Perhaps they decided the Rosebud area was far enough away from possible trouble. They were not too far, however, from the Blackfoot reserve. James and Eliza could not be sure where the Native people stood in relation to them. They may have found their promised land, but the times were still troubled and the future uncertain.

A Blackfoot named High Eagle approached James and Eliza soon after their arrival.[4] He was to become a friend and a great help to James and Eliza as they settled into their new surroundings. He told James where to find game and locate trees that could be cut into logs for their new home.

And so in 1885 they settled in what was to be for them the promised land. At Rosebud[5] they finished raising the family that accompanied them on their journey west. Eliza died in 1900 at the age of 65, James in 1904, at the age of 74. A gravestone marks their burial spot. It stands in the cemetery at Gleichen (Siding 12) where James and Eliza first set foot in Alberta. It was from Gleichen that James set out on his journey homeward during the Great Blizzard of 1887, the story that is the source of this story of discovery.

ered mushrooms hunt
Looking Back

CHAPTER 15

They Are Remembered

WHEREIN OUR ANCESTORS, DESPITE A LONG HISTORY
OF RACISM, ARE RESTORED TO A PLACE THEY SHOULD
ALWAYS HAVE HAD IN FAMILY LORE.

THE LEGACY OF JAMES AND ELIZA HAS NOT BEEN FORGOTTEN. Their brief stay in Red Deer is marked by a street named Wishart and by the Wishart Trail in the Gaetz Lakes Sanctuary. They are also remembered by an undesignated spruce tree which was planted by Shirley and me along the Wishart Trail. It stands near the promontory where James and Eliza's home was located. Shirley had previously found the spot where their log house had stood. Michael Dawe, the archivist at the Red Deer Museum, told her of its approximate location. The site is situated in a clearing in the aspen and spruce forest on the lip of a rise overlooking the Gaetz Lakes, which can be seen through the trees. The area has been preserved much like it must have been when James and Eliza first homesteaded there. We can thank the late Jack Gaetz for keeping it that way. Perhaps in the future, a plaque will be placed at the site of the old cabin, telling something of the Wishart story.

In Kerry Wood's little book *The Sanctuary*,[1] he recounts how Gaetz added the land he purchased from James and Eliza to his own to make a 230-acre sanctuary, all in its original wild state.

They Are Remembered

Vernon Wishart by the Wishart Trail, Red Deer
SHIRLEY WISHART

Wood writes:

> He [Jack Gaetz] *came here in 1885 and homesteaded the farmland to the east. One-quarter section of land he registered in his own name, while his mother added an additional 160 acres. Their holdings included part of the sanctuary land, but a larger portion had been already homesteaded by a pleasant man who was part Indian* [James Wishart]. *The half-breed wasn't too keen on becoming a farmer and had not done much ploughing, so he willingly sold his interests to Jack Gaetz.*

We know that James and Eliza, in fact, farmed in the Red River Settlement for years. They homesteaded at Red Deer Crossing in order to continue farming. The North West Rebellion ended on May 12, 1885. Even with an early spring, there would be little time to get on the land and do much farming and plowing with a single furrow plow, before the growing backlash began toward Métis, Native and Mixed-blood. While no mention is made of negative reaction locally arising from the Rebellion it is safe to conclude that James and Eliza would not depart such a promising homestead unless they were fearful of animosity toward them, so they made the decision to leave Red Deer Crossing. Wood continues:

What Lies Behind the Picture?

The homes of Mr. and Mrs. Jack Gaetz (centre) and
James and Eliza (right)
RED DEER AND DISTRICT MUSEUM AND ARCHIVES

Jack Gaetz and his mother, a charming and refined lady from Eastern Canada, moved into the log cabin the first settlers had built and found it made a cozy home.... To these two pioneers, the important feature of their new home site was the sylvan beauty of this area surrounding the two lakes. They decided to preserve the natural charm of the wild region near the ponds. Later, when Jack Gaetz married, his wife shared his love for the wilderness. Throughout the long years of settlement, they protected the beauty spot and saved the trees.... Canada could have done with more men and women like them! Pioneers with vision. People who loved beauty and who kept faith with their convictions that such an attractive wilderness should be preserved in nature's state.

    He and his wife willingly share it with the whole town and district.... We organized the first Natural History Society to be chartered in our province. Jack Gaetz gave the club permission to make this region a bird sanctuary, more than 30 years ago. Later, naturalists compiled a list of birds

They Are Remembered

that visited the area during migration times and residents nesting here. Nearly two hundred different varieties were named, while the wilderness has sheltered more than 30 species of animals ranging in size from two-inch shrews all the way up to giant bull moose.

[Jack Gaetz] and his mother lived in the half-breed's log cabin for years, adding an extra room after Jack married. Then, during the prosperous farming years when pioneering was over, they built a beautiful modern home next to the main road . . .

. . . Jack Gaetz died a few years ago, then his widow sold the farm. The provincial government bought it. There were fears that at last, the trees would be chopped down. But the area was officially declared a sanctuary a year ago [1951]. From now on it will be preserved in its natural state, just as Jack Gaetz kept it all the long years since 1885.

In addition to their recognition in *The Sanctuary*, James and Eliza are also remembered in the village of Rosebud as the first settlers in that area. As part of the commemoration of Canada's centennial, David Kenney, a family friend, built a log house using the logs from James and Eliza's home on what is now the Kenney farm. He furnished the house with period furniture, including a picture of James Wishart.

The Centenary project is near the home of the Kenney family. Since 1967 the Kenneys have welcomed visitors and acted as curators of the little museum. Their own house incorporates some of the walls of Dave and Maude Wishart's home where our father, Roy, was born. Below the hill upon which the log house is located, David Kenney erected a large granite stone on the original site of James and Eliza's home. The stone is a metre in height and bears a bronze plaque with the words:

THIS MARKS THE SITE OF
THE LOG HOME OF THE FIRST
SETTLERS OF THE ROSEBUD
VALLEY, JAMES AND ELIZA
WISHART, JUNE, 1885.

What Lies Behind the Picture?

Shirley Wishart by Heritage Marker, near Rosebud, Alberta
VERNON R. WISHART

They Are Remembered

Underneath the plaque are the words:

> PRESENTED JOINTLY BY
> WISHART DESCENDENTS,
> THE
> ROSEBUD HISTORICAL SOCIETY
> AND ALBERTA CULTURE.

On the hillside by the highway leading into Rosebud, there is a heritage marker placed by the Government of Alberta. It features a large photograph of the first settlers in the area, James and Eliza Wishart, supplied by Shirley Wishart and originally discovered in James and Eliza's family Bible.

Moving further back into the past, to the shadowed forests, inland rivers and the vast plains of what is now part of Canada, the figure of Isaac Batt emerges. His memory is preserved in the article, "Isaac Batt," written by Jennifer S. H. Brown in Volume IV of the *Dictionary of Canadian Biography*.

Isaac Batt and his country wife, our Native ancestor, had a daughter, Nestichio Batt who married James Spence. Nestichio and her way of life is highlighted in the Heritage Centre just outside of Elk Point, Alberta. The Centre is situated near the former sites of Buckingham House of the Hudson's Bay Company and Fort George of the North West Company.

From the pages of the past, another couple is remembered in the annals of the fur trade, William Flett and Saskatchewan. On September 11, 1997, the Edmonton Historical Board, at its Annual Recognition Awards, honored William A. Flett, among others, for their contribution to the City of Edmonton.

The evening began with a dinner followed by an awards ceremony. Acting Mayor, Terry Cavanaugh presented a scroll to family members of those honoured. Shirley, on behalf of the Wishart family received one of these Scrolls of Citation. Coincidently, Mr. Cavanaugh is a descendent of the Orcadian William Tomison, who was Chief Factor at Buckingham House where James Spence and Nestichio served.

The scroll includes the coat of arms of the City of Edmonton and reads as follows:

What Lies Behind the Picture?

THE CITY OF EDMONTON
RECOGNIZES THE
OUTSTANDING SERVICES OF
WILLIAM A. FLETT
IN PRESERVING OUR HERITAGE

Witnessed under my hand this 11th day of September
The year of our Lord, 1997
Signed: George F. Ferrand—Chair,
Edmonton Historical Board

Prior to the presentation of the scroll the following citation was read:

William A. Flett was born around 1762 in the Redland District of the Orkney Islands. Like many of his countrymen he signed on with the Hudson's Bay Company in 1782. His first posting was at York Factory when it was unfortunately captured by the French. Following a year as a prisoner, he returned to a reclaimed York Factory. Work with the Company included stints as a labourer, steersman and hunter. In 1793 he accompanied Peter Fidler as they explored the site for a Hudson's Bay post, which was later known as Edmonton House. Hudson's Bay records indicate that William Flett was a valued employee of the Company. He was an excellent marksman and buffalo hunter and also served as Master and Canoe Builder at Edmonton House on two separate occasions.[2] Flett finished out his career with the Company at Fort Edmonton in 1823. It can be truly said of William Flett, like many of his countrymen who worked for the Company, "They pulled the wilderness round them like a cloak, and wore its beauty like a crest."

A picture of William Flett, which Shirley drew based on photographs of later descendants, was mounted in a place of honour in the Heritage Centre of the Edmonton Historical Board and the City of Edmonton.[3]

WHAT BEGAN AS A BOLT OUT OF THE BLUE, A SINGLE LINE— "Eliza's knowledge of Indian medicine and surgery saved Jim's life"—has led our family to the discovery of a heritage we

They Are Remembered

never knew existed. As our father's closely kept secret of our Native roots was brought to light, it has illuminated a wonderful legacy of ancestors. The lives of Isaac Batt, James Spence, William Flett and Thomas Wishart, who ventured all to carve out a life in a rugged and formidable continent as fur traders, hunters, canoe men, boatmen and trusted servants of the Hudson's Bay Company, have now become part of our lives. Also a part of our lives are their wives: Native and Mixed-blood women, without whom these men would not have succeeded in their tasks or even survived. We think of the hardiness of Batt's wife, a Native woman who mothered Nestichio and whose name we do not know; the resourcefulness of Nestichio, the endurance of Saskatchewan, the spirituality of Eliza and the dependable loyalty of other wives, despite the harshness of the environment and the harsher reality of racism.

Closer to us now are our great-grandparents, James and Eliza, whose courage and determination enabled them to live through some of the most dramatic episodes in Western Canadian history, and within its several colliding cultures seek out a place to call home.

We started on this journey of discovery knowing very little. As each link in the chain has been uncovered, we have found people whom we are proud to call our own. They are not the kind of people studied by those who are interested only in the rich and the famous. They are ordinary people who are interesting in their own way. They lived in extraordinary times—the carving of Canada out of a wilderness, the country we call home.

CHAPTER 16

My Personal Journey

I HAVE BEEN ASKED WHETHER MY OWN ATTITUDES HAVE changed while telling the story of our fur trade and Native ancestry.

Let me begin with my Native ancestry. While I am proud of my aboriginal ancestry today, would I have been as proud as a boy?

One of my earliest childhood memories is in 1931 when I was four years old. Dad hired a Native guide to take us to a river west of Rocky Mountain House to do some fishing. Mom, Dad, Florence (Dad's sister), her husband and I followed our guide on horseback as he led us into wilderness country. I rode seated in the saddle in front of Dad. On reaching the location chosen by our guide, we set up our tents. He had previously placed his tent and family within sight of our camp.

While the grown-ups fished, I played with his son who was about my age. We made stick horses out of tree branches. For me, the important part of my stick horse was that it had something that resembled a horse's head. For my playmate, the tail was a more vital part than the head. His horse had a tail of leafy branches.

My Personal Journey

We rode our steeds with great abandon. I think we were too young for the idea of cowboys and Indians to have fastened in our minds. If it had, I think it didn't matter as we took turns pursuing one another. I suspect if someone said to me, "Did you know you were playing with an Indian?" I would have replied to the effect, "I didn't notice what he was. He was my friend."

As I grew into adolescence, my childhood innocence changed as I became aware of the stigma associated with being Native. Perhaps it came when I first heard of "The Indian List." It was a name that became attached to an interdict which was an official prohibition barring not only Natives but Whites who couldn't handle their liquor from the local beer parlor. The interdict, however, was arbitrarily applied to all Natives.

I grew up in a small town in central Alberta. I had a normal boyhood, cheered on while playing ball or hockey, working after school as a delivery boy, helping on farms in the summer to make extra money. There were those in the community and church who took a special interest in their young people. I thrived in the supportive atmosphere of home and community. When I was invited to go to Colorado College in the United States on a hockey scholarship, the local paper celebrated the fact. People in the community had a special send-off for me. I may be mistaken, but I think our town would have reflected the racism of the times and I would have been treated much differently if it was known I had Native ancestors. Certainly that was my father's conclusion.

I had little contact with Métis and Native people until, as part of my training for the ministry, I was sent to Kinuso, not far from the shores of Lesser Slave Lake in northern Alberta. The town was situated on a reserve but my contact was limited as the

---

A friend, whose brother was a Mountie with 25 years of experience in the service, asked his brother, "Is it true that Indians can't control their liquor?" To which he replied, "Yes, some control their liquor as badly as white people."

What Lies Behind the Picture?

Native people there were mostly Roman Catholics, and served by a resident priest. My friendships were with the Métis young men in the town and with whom I played baseball. Our main rivals were the Slave Lake team whose best players were Métis. On the ball field it didn't matter who you were as long as you could compete. Michael, the son of a respected Métis family, was in the youth group I started. I lent him my sports jacket for his graduation. He was the class valedictorian. Michael went on to become a lawyer. Every now and then I get a phone call from Michael who has kept in touch over the years.

After becoming an ordained minister, I served typical United Church congregations largely made up of white middle or upper-middle class people. While supporting most United Church policies[1] toward Native people, my only direct contact, until recently, with Native, Métis and Mixed-blood, have been fleeting encounters, and with those who came by the church, usually needing money for liquor or food. This experience made me painfully aware of what happens to many people who have been marginalized by the rest of society through generations of discrimination.

In 1955, I was to come in direct personal contact unknowingly with a Mixed-blood, my grandfather. Until then I had never met my grandfather, David Wishart. Our father spoke little of him. Perhaps it was too painful.

Dad was born in 1905 in Redland, Alberta, 100 kilometres northeast of Calgary. His family moved to Gleichen, 50 kilometres south, where Dave ran a livery stable, hiring out space for horses and providing transportation for land seekers during the rush for land.[2]

Grandfather Dave was a heavy drinker. He was generous with his friends but not an ideal husband and father. With the end of the land boom and the advent of the automobile, the livery business died a natural death and Dave went broke.[3] When the livery barn burnt down, any remaining business associated with it went as well. Dave was devastated. He left his wife Maude and their two children, Florence, age 16 and Roy, our Dad, age 10 and went to southern Alberta to work on ranches and eventually to take up the life of a sheepherder.[4] He may have felt the isolated life would help him kick his drinking habits.

In May 1952, I completed my studies for the ministry. I was to be ordained at the annual conference of the church. The venue was Lethbridge, Alberta. The last word we had of our grandfather's whereabouts was he was residing in Lethbridge. I was determined to find him. My search took me to several rooming houses with no success until someone said, "There is a David Wishart in the hospital."

I will never forget the moment I entered his hospital room and introduced myself. There were tears. Grandfather was an old man now of 85 years. One of his legs had been amputated below the knee. The rugged countenance was still there. There was the look in his eyes of a man who had regrets but was at peace with himself.

I informed Dad and Mom of my discovery. Surprisingly, Dad was not upset. If anything I sensed he was pleased that the contact had been made. As I reflect back on my conversation with Dad, he must have been listening very carefully to determine whether or not his father had disclosed that which he had concealed from his children. Probably, when Dave met me, he decided that he too would not reveal the secret. Perhaps he believed that Dad had already done so.

The following summer I visited him again. This time Shirley joined me. He was in a senior citizens' residence and came out to meet us supported by a cane, for by now he had an artificial leg. As Shirley and I look back on our meeting with Granddad, it never occurred to us that there was more to his story.

Not long afterwards, I went to do graduate work in the United States. Shirley kept in contact with Dave through regular correspondence. Not once did he mention that he was a Mixed-blood.

Out of deference to his mother, Dad never visited his father. Grandfather died at the age of 88 in May 1956 at St. Michael's Hospital, Lethbridge, just 15 minutes before Dad, Mother and Shirley reached his bedside.[5] Shirley and I were not aware that we had been in contact with our Native heritage through our

What Lies Behind the Picture?

grandfather until 1962 when the story of the Great Blizzard of 1887 came to light.

A recent and memorable encounter took place while I was visiting a person in palliative care. I noticed that Harold Cardinal was a patient in an adjoining room. The name rang a bell but I was not sure in what way. I took the liberty of visiting him and found him reticent to talk about himself. After my brief visit, I went to the library and discovered he had written a book, *The Unjust Society*, which helped to stimulate the national Aboriginal rights movement and inspired young Natives to take pride in their culture. Cardinal led the Indian Association of Alberta for nine years and had been an articulate spokesperson in opposing any government action designed to dismantle the reserve system and assimilate Native people into White culture. When I returned a couple of weeks later his room was empty and I was told he had returned to his reserve. He died on June 3, 2005.

It was not, however, until I began researching the history of our fur trade and Native ancestors that I became fully aware of how, from the beginning, the cards were stacked against Native, Métis and Mixed-blood people. I recalled a dear friend, Peter Paris, an African-American Professor of Christian Social Ethics at Princeton Theological Seminary, saying to me in the fifties that in many ways the situation of Native people in Canada was worse than that of the Blacks in the United States. The history of our treatment of Native, Métis and Mixed-blood people is a disturbing story and one which most people choose to ignore. There continues to be little knowledge of their situation in Canada and even less interest. Particularly sad is the tendency among some to blame the victim—justifying inequality by finding defects in the victims of inequality—or to adopt the attitude: "Why can't they be like us?" We have not rooted out the racial paternalism and racism of the past.

I mentioned in the Prologue that in the summer of 1993, Shirley, through her many contacts with fur trade relatives, organized a "Batt, Spence, Flett, Halcro, Wishart Reunion Week-End" at Elk Point, Alberta. Over 50 persons attended from as far away as Manitoba and British Columbia. On Sunday, I led the

My Personal Journey

Service of Worship. Louise Crane, a relative of Peter Fidler and his Native wife, opened the worship with a smudge of sweet grass. During my sermon I said:

> How each of us has made the linkage with our roots in the past, and have incorporated them into the present, varies. Some of you have been aware of your roots and have made them a part of your personal story and identity. Some of you have been aware of your roots but have been willing, only recently, to claim them as your own. Others, like our own family, were aware of our old country roots but not aware of our Native heritage. This was largely because of the fear among our parents of social stigma. Part of our being here is to release and redeem that fear and pain as we claim as part of our heritage, not only our Orcadian roots, but also our Native roots.

As I was about to complete this manuscript for publication, I attended a unique gathering of those who were proud to claim their Native heritage. In August 2005 a Red River Descendants' Reunion was held at Lower Fort Garry to mark its 175th anniversary. The fort is about 20 kilometres outside of Winnipeg and was built by Governor Simpson in 1830. Constructed of stone from the area, it has since been restored to its original setting. It was an ideal location for over 200 descendants of fur trade families. They came from all over Canada, and as far away as Scotland, France, Holland, Japan and Alaska to claim their roots and share their stories. The organizers of the reunion provided an opportunity to find and trace ancestors through genealogical and archival sources. Lectures, films, tours, and presenters in period costume ushered us into the life of the early fur traders and settlers. It was a stimulating and informative experience.

I talked to many people who like myself were present because they had discovered quite by accident their Native heritage. One woman said that her brother was of darker complexion than the rest of the family. He was called "Half-breed" by school-mates. Angered by these taunts, he got into fights and she, though smaller, tried to protect him. She said they had no inkling of their Native background. One day a knock came at their door. When they opened it, there stood a gentleman who introduced

What Lies Behind the Picture?

himself as Charles Denney. Denney was a well-known and respected genealogist who, like a detective searching for missing persons, sought out those who had Native ancestry in order to complete his many genealogical trees. His visit prompted a search of his massive files as well as HBC archives. As a result, she and her sister were able to trace their roots back to the early fur traders and their Native wives; and their descendants among whom was the wife of John Norquay, the first Mixed-blood Premier of Manitoba.

Other people spoke of "Grandmother having a secret." One person recounted how her grandmother would not go out in the sun for a duration of time for fear of turning a deeper brown and so revealing her Native identity.

Another interesting story was that of Virginia Barter who, over coffee, related to me her discovery. She had no idea of her Mixed-blood identity until she was viewing a National Film Board documentary with the title, "Fiddlers of James Bay". One of the Cree fiddle players in the film was from Fort George on the eastern shores of James Bay. In the film he relates in Cree how his great-grandfather had come to Fort George from overseas to work with the Hudson's Bay Company. He held up a picture and proudly pointed to his great-grandparents. Virginia said she could hardly believe her eyes "and they were my great-great-grandparents too!" She embraced that discovery and has launched a fascinating journey to uncover her family history.

For me the reunion was not only a stimulus to meet people who had discovered and claimed their Aboriginal roots, but it also provided an opportunity to walk where my forebears walked. I strolled along the edge of the Red River: the river where my fur trade ancestors transported HBC furs and supplies by canoe and York boat, the river which tied the Settlement together, the river which supplied water for drinking and washing, for harvesting of fish, the river that was a highway in both summer and winter. I visited the parishes where the descendants of the fur traders once worked their farms. And, I sought out the gravesites, now unmarked because of the elements and the passage of time, where my ancestors were laid to rest. Having made

My Personal Journey

this pilgrimage, I felt I could conclude my manuscript and hand it over for publication.

This book has been a work in progress over several years. It has been a labour of love as well as a journey of discovery. As I followed our ancestors across a continent, I have a sharpened sense of being a Canadian. These early fur traders and their families of mixed ancestry left a lasting imprint on Canadian society. They forged "a social conscience and experience distinct from our American cousins."[6]

In my reading and contacts, I have visited historical events that were never taught in school or if they were they were passed over quickly. For example, how many of us know that 1885 is a hallmark year not only in Western but also in Canadian history? Duck Lake, Battleford, Frog Lake and Batoche were not only events that transpired on the battlefield but also shaped attitudes and policies that have been the source of continuing tensions within communities, and even within families.

Originally, this manuscript was intended only for family and friends. I was pleasantly surprised when the Central Alberta Historical Society felt it warranted a wider readership. Concerned that it be an acceptable and well-researched piece of work, I sent initial drafts to several friends knowledgeable in fur trade history—Sylvia Van Kirk, Donna Sutherland, and Peter Melnyky—who made helpful suggestions, all of which entailed more work on my part. I became painfully aware of one of Pierre Berton's commandments for writers: "Read! Read! Read! Write! Write! Write! Rewrite! Rewrite! Rewrite!"[7]

When I began to despair whether it was worth the effort, I reminded myself of the words of my friend, Bill Acheson, Professor Emeritus of History at the University of New Brunswick:

> *What a wonderful heritage record you have managed to assemble! Most of us end up with a modest farmer or woods worker who spent a lifetime on the back forty—and that's assuming we can find any record at all. Your forebears were roaming an entire continent doing the things that are written about in the great novels of exploration . . . In a sense,*

What Lies Behind the Picture?

given the nature of the plains community in the eighteenth and early nineteenth centuries, your family is synonymous with that community.

Bill's words may have been coloured by our friendship (even historians are not totally objective), but they were enough to keep me at the task.

In the course of my research I was to discover strands that carried me far afield. In particular, I found relatives Mary Ballard in Oklahoma and Mary Ellen Dean Williamson in the state of Washington, who provided me with important material on Thomas and Barbara Wishart and the children who accompanied them; and, more recently, second cousins in Montana, Jolene Jacobson and Judy Herman, who are descendants of Herb Wishart, the youngest son of James and Eliza. But for this book, I needed to keep the focus on the Canadian story. It helped to let go of these important pieces of information knowing that they will be picked up by Shirley and woven into another more comprehensive work.

I hope this book will be a stimulus to others to search out their ancestors and claim them for their own. In Canada we are in danger of losing our past and what makes us Canadians. The impact of a technological and consumer-oriented society creates an ethos which increasingly severs us from our past. As a result, we do not seem to know who we are, where we are going, or how we are connected with the past. We are uncertain of our unique Canadian identity.

It is my hope that many of you who read this book will reclaim your past and own it; write it down; and organize family reunions. You will discover many elders in the family who have three or four generations in their heads. Good journeying.

EPILOGUE

Defining Moments

OUR FATHER GREW UP IN AN ETHOS OF RACISM, WHICH can be traced in our family history to the Red River Settlement of the 1800s and the events following the North West Rebellion in 1885. These defining moments reached forward to him as a boy in his own home and community.

Racism followed him in later years like an ever-pursuing, venomous snake that might strike at any moment. Dad dreaded that wherever he went he might hear, "Mind yourself, he has Indian blood." He tried to escape the stigma of racial profiling by relocating, hoping it would not be able to follow him or his family. But always it carried the risk of resurfacing, in varied places and forms: exclusion from the lodge, neighborhood parties, snide comments in the poolroom, and sudden silence in the stores when he and Mother came to shop. Who can blame those like our father who wanted to distance themselves from childhood memories of discrimination? In Dad's case, he moved to central Alberta, where he entered the mainstream of white society. He had a job, a family and the rewards of hard work.

We have a touching photo of our father. It was taken shortly

What Lies Behind the Picture?

after my wife Jo and I returned from our studies in the States in 1958 with James, our first child. It is a family picnic. Dad is sitting and contemplating his first blond and blue-eyed grandchild. There is pensiveness in his expression. We wonder now what thoughts and emotions were going through his mind? Was he saying to himself, "I see no hint of Native blood in my grandson." Dad died seven months later believing he had protected his family from the shadow of racism.

In one sense, he did succeed. While growing up we were spared from being ashamed of who we were; never experiencing the anxiety of racial prejudice; never having to define ourselves by another's disregard. By the time we came to know about our Native heritage, we were well established in our chosen vocations. We no longer feared the imprint with which some might want to brand us. Instead, we embraced our roots, recognizing that we were richer because of them.

We proudly bear in our bodies the genes of the Hudson's Bay Company fur traders and their Native wives. We celebrate the fact that we are the same distance from Isaac Batt as from his Native wife. We do not want to be drawn away from one of the most precious legacies we have, *where we came from and how we got to be where we are.*

Will there be a time when we can celebrate a deliverance from racism? I look to the day "when former things have passed away"[1] erasing the last vestiges of racism and exclusion whispered in a hospital room, "They are Wisharts, Half-breeds you know."

Acknowledgements

As a family, we are grateful to the late John J. Martin and his book, *The Rosebud Trail*. His account of The Blizzard of 1887 was our first indication that we possessed Mixed-blood ancestry.

We are also grateful to the late Charles Denney, a genealogist and friend. He provided Shirley with material which added impetus to the search for our roots. Mr. Denney also gave me a copy of Annie L. Gaetz's book, *The Park Country: A History of Red Deer and District,* which provided valuable historical background for James and Eliza Wishart's time at Red Deer Crossing. Mr. E. L. Meeres kindly gave Shirley permission to use material from his book *Homesteads That Nurtured A City,* which documents James and Eliza's arrival at Siding 12 (later to be named Gleichen, Alberta) and their journey to and settlement near Red Deer Crossing.

We wish to express our appreciation to historian Peter Melnycky, who has kindly shared his research on James Spence Sr.; and to Michael Payne, Head of Research and Publications, both of Alberta Historic Sites. Peter and Michael read the initial draft and made helpful suggestions. A personal thank you to Donna Sutherland, historian and author, for reading the initial draft and since offering information about the Red River Settlement, the fur-trade and Native culture; and to Bill Acheson, Professor Emeritus of the History Department, the University of New Brunswick, for reading the initial draft and giving insightful and encouraging comments. I wish also to express my appreciation to Allison Kydd, editor and writer, for her careful reading of the manuscript and catching grammar and stylistic mistakes.

We wish also to express our thanks to Michael Dawe, Archivist for the City of Red Deer, who has taken a special interest in preserving the memory of James and Eliza Wishart. We also wish to express our appreciation to Cam Finlay for sharing his research on William Flett and urging us to make Flett's connection with Fort Edmonton, and to the late Lois Porter, a past member of the Edmonton Historical Board for bringing to the Board the story, "Fort, Flett and Family," which Shirley and I wrote; and to Carolina Roemmich, archivist and researcher, for alerting me to George Simpson's journal where he speaks of Saskatchewan. We owe a real debt of gratitude to David Kenney and his family for the 1967 Centennial project, which helped to preserve the memory of James and Eliza. We are also indebted to Gordon C. Fielder and David G. Fielder for the information they have shared with us of William Flett Jr. and Saskatchewan. I would like to acknowledge my debt to Mary Dawe who gave me confidence as a writer and to the encouragement of the Minerva writing group who listened patiently to many excerpts as the manuscript was in progress and made constructive comments. A special thank you to Jim Fargey for his continued interest and support as the manuscript progressed.

Among those I wish to acknowledge are family members: my brother Bill Wishart, a retired wild-life biologist who carefully read the manuscript and offered advice on fauna. He also found Hudson's Bay Company archival material which documented William Flett's term in charge of Fort Edmonton; his wife Pat for her advice on flora; their son, David Wishart, who saved me from

Acknowledgements

major computer headaches; and our daughter, Beth MacKenzie, who suggested wording and improvements in style.

At Shirley's suggestion, I have done a considerable search by Internet for information about Thomas and Barbara Wishart. This has led to the discovery of relatives and friends in the States who have graciously shared information about Thomas and Barbara Wishart and their family after they left the Red River Settlement in Manitoba and settled in Iowa. Among these, we are deeply indebted to newly found relatives, Mary Dean Heller Williamson, Mary Ballard and Dianna Mortensen, as well as a very helpful friend, Sharyl Farrell. All have shared a special interest in this project.

I wish to express my deep appreciation and indebtedness to our friend Sylvia Van Kirk, a recognized historian of fur-trade society and the author of what has become a classic, *"Many Tender Ties": Women in Fur-Trade Society, 1670-1870.* Sylvia believed that the story of our ancestry is fascinating and should be told in a way that truly honours our heritage. Her critical eye not only sharpened the historical background and accuracy of the text but suggested major revisions which led to further research. Where faults obstinately remain, they are mine alone.

Special mention should be made of the Hudson's Bay Company Archives, Archives of Manitoba in Winnipeg, and their staff. The archives are a rich source of information about the fur-trade and the staff has willingly made that information available as well as photos and maps. A great big thank you to the Central Alberta Joint Publication Committee for their patience in waiting for the final draft, in particular Don Hepburn for his encouragement and gentle nudging, and Bill Baergen for his careful reading of the final draft. The Committee's selection of Linda Goyette, well-known author and journalist, as editor has underlined their concern that their publications be of high quality.

Finally, I wish to express my gratitude to Jo, my wife, for her proofreading, encouragement, support, patience and sage advice over the last five years, which has taken up much of my time which was really her time, too.

Notes

PROLOGUE
What Lies Behind The Picture

[1] Naomi Jackson Groves, *A.Y.'s Canada* (Toronto/ Vancouver: Clarke, Irwin & Co. 1968), 128.

[2] John J. Martin, *The Rosebud Trail* (Rosebud: Martin, 1962), 77. Betty-Rose Jenkins, ed.

[3] Shirley Wishart, *From the Red to the River of Many Rosebuds: Akokiniskway* (Calgary: Wishart, 1983), 10.

[4] Martin, *The Rosebud Trail*, 75.

[5] Ibid.

[6] Ibid.

[7] Ibid. It was not unusual for persons caught in blizzards and suffering from cold and fatigue to experience voices.

[8] Ibid., 76. Martin describes Eliza's medicine bag "as full of roots hung high upon a spruce log. After selecting the right root she chewed it to a pulp and placed it directly on the wound and wrapped it in buckskin."

[9] Millicent Martin, the wife of John Martin, shared this

Notes

personal reminiscence.

[10] Metis is the modern form of the word *Métis*, but both, along with *Michif*, a blend of French and Plains Cree, refer to a specific identity and culture. For the choice of *Mixed-blood*, see Sylvia Van Kirk, *Many Tender Ties* (Winnipeg: Watson and Dwyer, 1980), 255 n. 8. Van Kirk cites Jennifer S. H. Brown, "Linguistic Solitudes in the Fur Trade: Some Changing Social Categories and their Implications" in C. M. Judd and A. J. Ray, eds., *Old Trails and New Directions: Papers of the Third North American Fur Trade Conference* (Toronto, 1980) for a discussion of both contemporary and modern terms and the problems associated with their usage.

CHAPTER 1
Isaac Batt and his Native Wife

[1] For a biographical sketch of Isaac Batt see Jennifer S. H. Brown, "Isaac Batt," *Dictionary of Canadian Biography, Vol. 4, 1771 to 1800* (Toronto: University of Toronto Press, 1979), 46–48. A brief biography of Isaac Batt appears in J. B. Tyrrell, ed., *Journals of Samuel Hearne and Philip Turnor* (Toronto: Champlain Society, 1934), 5 n.2 and there are frequent references to him in the *Hudson's Bay Record Society's Cumberland House Journal and Inland Journals 1775-1782*, First Series, 1775–79, and Second Series, 1779–82, eds., E. E. Rich and A. M. Johnson (London, 1951 and 1952). References to a daughter of Batt named Nestichio will be found in A. M. Johnson, ed., *Saskatchewan Journals and Correspondence Edmonton House, 1795-1800, Chesterfield House 1800-1802.* (London: Hudson's Bay Record Society (HBRS), 1967) 17 n.1. Isaac Batt's brother James was also in the service of the Company. Frequent references are made to him in the *Cumberland House Journal and Inland Journals*. See Second Series, September 1776, 347 n.19.

[2] I am indebted to Donna Sutherland for this description of the Swampy Cree: "The term Swampy Cree is most specific to the Cree people residing in the Hudson and James Bay lowlands. The Swampy Cree people use the term Omushkego—'People of the Muskeg'—to identify themselves."

What Lies Behind the Picture?

³Anthony Henday, quoted by Clifford Wilson in *Dictionary of Canadian Biography Vol. III, 1740 to 1770*, 287. Henday's original journal was never found but four copies survive in the HBC Archives in Winnipeg. B.239/a/40 contains a copy sent from York Factory by James Isham in 1775 which is inaccurate in some respects but ends with a strong plea for inland expansion. The claims of Henry Kelsey, also travelling for the HBC in 1690–91 and Henday that they were the "first white men" to see what were to become the Prairie provinces is not true as French traders had been travelling west before Kelsey.

⁴A.11–115 fo. 23.

⁵The capitalization of "Native" is a stylistic change used by many Native writers.

⁶Sylvia Van Kirk, *"Many Tender Ties",* 37.

⁷Tyrrell, *Journals*, 6.

⁸A.6/10/107–113.

⁹Tyrrell, *Journals*, 6.

¹⁰William Tomison, Chief Factor at Cumberland House, records on Sept. 22, 1777, that "Isaac Batt also set off for the said country [Buffalo country] accompanied with his family; He has Ammunition &c. for his support in the Winter time also Powder, Ball &c. to kill Buffalo for Food for our men when they arrive there next spring, and has promised to get a large Canoe made." See *Cumberland House Journal and Inland Journals,* First series, 190.

¹¹Richard Glover, ed., *Samuel Hearne, A Journey from Prince of Wales Fort in Hudson's Bay to the Northern Ocean 1795* (Toronto: 1958), 238.

¹²Shirley Wishart citing Jennifer S. H. Brown & Robert Brightman, *"The Orders of the Dreamed": George Nelson on Cree and Northern Ojibwa Religion and Myth* (Winnipeg, 1988), 114, 123, 175.

¹³Shirley Wishart, "Circles Within Circles: The Linkage of Hudson's Bay Company Fur Trade Families in Rupert's Land," *Rupert's Land Colloquium Papers* (Edmonton, 1994), 291.

¹⁴Matonabbee, Samuel Hearne's trusted guide, on the importance of Native women: " . . . when all the men are heavy

Notes

laden, they can neither hunt nor travel to any considerable distance; and in case they meet with success in hunting, who is to carry the produce of their labours? ... [women] were made for labour; one of them can carry, or haul, as much as two men can do. They also pitch our tents, make and mend our clothing, keep us warm at night; and in fact, there is no such thing as travelling any considerable distance, or for any length of time, in this country, without [women]." See Samuel Hearne, *A Journey from Prince of Wales Fort*, 62.

[15] Van Kirk, *Many Tender Ties*, 38.
[16] Brown, Isaac Batt, 47.
[17] Ibid., 47.
[18] *Hudson's Bay Company, Vol. I, 1670-1870, Vol. 2, 1763-1870* (London: HBRS, 58–61). See also *Cumberland House Journal and Inland Journals*, 1951. Also HBCA, B.239/a/71 and A.1/44, fo. 79–79d.
[19] Brown, Isaac Batt, 47.
[20] Tyrell, *Journals*, 6. Isaac's House, according to some sources, was also known as Fort aux Trembles. The nearest modern community would be Cronlid, Saskatchewan.
[21] Rich and Johnson, *Cumberland House Journal and Inland Journals*, 16–17, 112, 116, 149.
[22] Brown, Isaac Batt, 47.
[23] HBCA, B.3/a/73, fo. 15d.
[24] HBCA, A.11/116, fo. 22.
[25] Rich and Johnson quoting E. T. Seton, 17 n 1.
[26] Brown, Isaac Batt, 47.
[27] Ibid., 47
[28] Clifford Spence of Brentwood Bay, British Columbia, who is also a descendant of Isaac Batt, visited Pike's Peak and while there met a Gros Ventre Native from the United States who said that he had come to visit the site where his people had murdered Isaac Batt (Source: Clifford Spence.) Peter Fidler's journal, 1792 has this account of Batt's murder: "... this man [Batt] was inhumanly massacred by some Blackfoot in the summer of 1791 on his way into barren ground to kill buffalo, in company with John Thompson—who they suffered to escape unhurt—

What Lies Behind the Picture?

Isaac speaking a little of the Blackfoot language—and generally having a small assortment of medicines he used to frighten the Indians so much—by them that at last they shot him on that account—large payments were offered to that nation to any person who would deliver up the person that committed that atrocious deed, but none would pay the least attention to the offer." HBCA, Reel 4M4 E.3.1.

[29] Brown, Isaac Batt, 48.

[30] Ibid., 47.

[31] HBCA, Reel 5 A. 144. In some accounts Basquias is associated with The Pas, east of Cumberland House.

[32] London Correspondence, August 25, 1777. While there is a record of the London correspondence the archival reference HBCA, A.6/12 fo. 54. may not be correct or was copied incorrectly. I am grateful to Kathy Mallet, archivist at the HBCA for the hours she spent in trying to locate the correct archival reference for the August 25, 1777 correspondence.

CHAPTER 2
Nestichio Batt and James Spence

[1] I am indebted to Peter Melnycky for this chapter and his fine research on James Spence Senior. Sources for many archival references to James Spence Senior are to be found in his bio-file, HBCA. There are frequent references to Spence in the *Cumberland House Journal and Inland Journals* edited by E. E. Rich and A. M. Johnson. See page 241 and May 30, 1775, Oct. 5, and April 16, 1776, Sept. 22, 1777 and June 25 & 26, 1778 describing his work as a Company labourer. Most of the entries where Spence is mentioned are by William Tomison, Chief Factor at Cumberland House.

[2] Peter Melnycky, "Spence of Buckingham House: A Case Study of Genealogy and Fur Trade Biography," *Rupert's Land Colloquium Papers* (Winnipeg, 1994), 196, quoting Sir John Sinclair, ed., *The Statistical Account of Scotland 1791-1799, Vol xix: Orkney & Shetland Reprint* (East Ardsley: EP Publishing Limited, 1978), 14.

[3] Ibid., quoting Sinclair, 9–10.

Notes

[4] See Chapter 3, pp. 66–67, for a description of the position of Master.

[5] Melnycky, 196 citing Tyrell, *Journals,* 48.

[6] Ibid., 197.

[7] Ibid.

[8] Arthur Herman, *How the Scots Invented the Modern World* (New York: Three Rivers Press, 2001), 22–23.

[9] HBCA, Reel 1M256, B.239/b/51 fo.15–17. York Factory Correspondence Book (1791).

[10] Ibid.

[11] The result of Peter Melnycky's research is illustrated at the fine Interpretive Centre near Elk Point, Alberta. The Centre marks the location of Buckingham House and Fort George of the North West Company. With the aid of others, Melnycky has established, within the palisades of Buckingham House, gravesites, including that of James Spence.

[12] Tomison, an Orcadian, was the Chief Factor and the first inland officer of the HBC. On the retirement of Humphrey Marten as the superintendent of York Factory in 1786, Tomison was appointed by the Company to succeed him. He was, however, to reside inland because the majority of the trade was obtained from there, "with full Powers to act as he shall judge best for promoting the Trade." See Tyrell, ed., *Journals of Samuel Hearne and Philip Turnor,* Appendix A, 585.

[13] Van Kirk, *Many Tender Ties,* 96–97.

[14] Wishart, "Circles within Circles," 1994, 294.

[15] Jennifer S. H. Brown cites Ross Malchom's quote of Peter Fidler: "An Indian woman at a house is particularly useful in making shoes, cutting line, netting snow shoes, cleaning and stretching Beaver skin etc., that the Europeans are not acquainted with." See *Dictionary of Canadian Biography, Vol. IV,* 684–85.

[16] Melnycky, *Rupert's Land Colloquium, 1994:* 199 citing John Nicks, "The Diary of a Young Fur Trader: The 1789–1790 Journal of Thomas Staynor," in Lewis H. Thomas, ed., *Essays on Western History in Honour of Lewis Gwynne Thomas* (Edmonton: University of Alberta Press, 1976), 24–25. This attack on humans is highly unusual. Until recently there have

What Lies Behind the Picture?

been only three or four known attacks and of these only one was a rabid wolf. In 2005 a wolf killed a geological engineering student working in a mining camp in the northeastern corner of Saskatchewan. See *Maclean's* Magazine (December 2005), 48.

[17]Ibid., 200. See also Tomison's letter to James Spence from Edmonton House, Nov. 12, 1795, in *Saskatchewan Journals and Correspondence,* 48.

[18]HBCA, A.30/6 fo. 78; B.24/a/3; A.36/12.

[19]Jennifer S. H. Brown, *Strangers in Blood: Fur Trade Company Families in Indian Land* (Vancouver: University of British Columbia Press, 1985), 48. Spence's Will, dated 6 Nov. 1795, was proved in Prerogative Court of Canterbury on 25 November 1796 (HBCA B.24/a/3, Nov. 1795 and HBCA A.16/32.) Kathy Mallet, archivist at the HBCA, Winnipeg, kindly showed my sister, Shirley, and me James Spence Senior's Will, which is placed in a special room in the Archives for ancient documents. The room is kept at 14 degrees centigrade.

[20]HBCA, A.6/16, 28 May 1800.

[21]HBCA, A.36/1A fo. 1, entitled "Annuitants" on cover: "Drs James, Andrew, George, Margaret and Mother Spence/James Spence" GL fo. 130 letter of May 31, 1806.

[22]Melnycky, *Colloquium,* 202.

[23]See Chapter 9 for description of the Seven Oaks Massacre.

[24]J. M. Bumsted, *Trials & Tribulations: The Red River Settlement and the Emergence of Manitoba, 1811-1870* (Winnipeg: Great Plains Publication, 2003), 11–35. Further information on Lord Selkirk and the Red River colonists and the impact they had on the North West Company was given in a lecture by Dr. Bumsted at the Reunion of Descendants of Red River Settlers at the 175th Anniversary of Lower Fort Garry, August 2005.

[25]Melynicky, *Colloquium,* 203.

[26]Spence Family Archives, C. A. Kipling, "Genealogy of Spence Family" SFA care of Clifford Spence, Brentwood Bay, British Columbia, 1992.

[27]Stone or Stoney was the name given to the Assiniboine who heated water by putting a hot stone in a buffalo hide con-

tainer of water.

CHAPTER 3
A Country Marriage

[1] Sources for many archival references to William Flett and Saskatchewan are to be found in the William A. Flett bio-file HBCA. The name Flett is one of the earliest recorded Orkney names. It comes from the old Norse word Flagth, meaning witch. Like Spence, it is a name now found all over North America.

[2] HBCA, B.239/a/80 Reel 1M159 York Factory Journal 1773–1782.

[3] HBCA, B.239/1/81 Reel 1M159.

[4] Tyrrell, *Journals*, 584.

[5] An HBC officer describing life in Rupert's Land wrote: "... Nine months of winter, varied by three of rain and mosquitoes."

[6] Brown, *Strangers in Blood*, 27–28.

[7] Nicks, *Journal of Thomas Staynor*, 17. Chief Factor William Tomison described Flett as "the only one at this house [Buckingham House] that can kill a beast when needed." See *Saskatchewan Journals and Correspondence*, 60.

[8] HBCA, E.3/2. 70–75 Reel 4M4. "Journal of a Journey by Land along the North side of the Saskatchewan River & up it to the Tea Sturgeon or Red Willow River—by Peter Fidler in 1793."

[9] Ibid.

[10] Ibid.

[11] Ibid.

[12] *Saskatchewan Journals and Correspondence*, 14.

[13] Ibid., xxxi.

[14] George Heath MacDonald, *Fort Augustus-Edmonton: North West Trails and Traffic* (Edmonton: Douglas Print Co., 1954), 27.

[15] A cairn has since been erected northeast of present day Fort Saskatchewan and overlooking the site of the two rival companies.

[16] Sir George Simpson, *Narrative of a Journey Round the World: During the Years 1841-42, Vol. I* (London: Henry Colburn Publication), 89.

What Lies Behind the Picture?

[17] See also G. H. Armstrong, *The Origin and Meaning of Place Names in Canada* (Toronto: MacMillan, 1972), 257.

[18] Brown, *Strangers in Blood*, 50. See Chapter 1, n. 6 for the recognition of the legitimacy of such marriages. For a more detailed discussion of marriage with Native women see Chapter 3, and Van Kirk, *Many Tender Ties*, Chapter 2.

[19] Van Kirk, *Many Tender Ties*, 63. Van Kirk is speaking here of the HBC's inland exploration in the earlier years by men like Henday and Hearne. I would add Isaac Batt. It is safe to say that by the time of James Spence and William Flett there was an equal dependence on Native woman. See Van Kirk, *Many Tender Ties*, Chapter 3, for an excellent documentation of the important role of Native women in inland exploration and the fur trade.

[20] For an excellent discussion of the history and the nature of buffalo see Lu Carbyn, *The Buffalo Wolf* (Washington and London: Smithsonian Books, 2003), 34.

[21] William Tomison, while Chief Factor at Buckingham House, describes Flett as "useful in hunting buffalo." HBCA, B.49/f/2, fo. 3. After a kill the hunter would throw down a cloth, or something distinctive, next to the animal as a mark of ownership.

[22] It was not unusual for a fur trader to marry a young Native woman. David Thompson, the well-known surveyor and astronomer, married Charlotte Small whose mother was Cree. Charlotte was 14 and Thompson was 29.

[23] Olive Dickason, *The New Peoples: Being and Becoming Metis in North America*, edited by Jacqueline Peterson and Jennifer S. H. Brown (Winnipeg: University of Manitoba Press, 1985), 24.

[24] Van Kirk, *Many Tender Ties*, 37.

[25] Ibid.

[26] Ibid.

[27] For a description of the importance of the York boat see Dennis F. Johnson, *Inland Armada: The York Boats of the Hudson's Bay Company*, (Selkirk, Manitoba: Lower Fort Garry Association, 2005).

[28] Herman, *How The Scots Invented The Modern World*, 22–23.

[29] Van Kirk, *Many Tender Ties*, 61.

Notes

CHAPTER 4
Flett's Journal at Edmonton House

[1] *Edmonton District Journal for 1819,* Provincial Archives of Alberta (PAA), Reel 1M49 B.60/a/18. The entries in the Journal follow as closely as possible Flett's handwriting and punctuation. The purpose is to give the reader a sense of life at Edmonton House during the spring and summer months.

[2] HBCA, B.60/a/9.

[3] HBCA, B.60/a/20.

[4] PAA Reel 1M49 B.60/a/21. Flett would 58, not 55. It is interesting to note that after 38 years of service to the Company Flett's annual wage was £40. This is an increase from his beginning salary, but it is in marked contrast to the salaries of the Chief Traders and Chief Factors. In addition to their wages they received 40 per cent of the Company's net profit each year. The profit was subdivided into shares with one share going to each of the Chief Traders and two shares going to each of the Chief Factors. In 1834 this amounted to £400 and £800 respectively.

[5] Copies of Saskatchewan and William Flett's burial registers have been obtained from the Anglican Church of Canada's archives.

[6] Van Kirk, *Many Tender Ties,* 45. The designation "reputed" was often used by traders and clergy to acknowledge that a church marriage had not occurred (Brown, *Strangers in Blood*), 145–146. Nevertheless, marriage "according to the custom of the country" was recognized as a bona fide marital union. From 1867 to 1872 the courts in Quebec ruled in what was to become known as "The Great Connolly Case" that the marriage of William Connolly (Irish) and Miyo Nipi (Native), "according to the custom of the country," was a legal marriage and the offspring of the marriage were legitimate children, and entitled to a share of Connolly's estate. See John Adams, *Old Square-Toes and His Lady,* (Victoria: Horsdal & Shubert, 2001), 181–185.

[7] Brown, xiv-xv.

[8] Ibid., 151.

[9] Van Kirk, *Many Tender Ties,* 201.

[10] Ibid.

What Lies Behind the Picture?

CHAPTER 5
Saskatchewan: A Venerable Sojourner

[1] HBCA, A.36/6, fo. 130; E.4/1a, fo. 55; E.4/2, fo. 145; E.5/1, fo. 4 through E.5/8 fo. 8.

[2] William J. Betts, "From Red River to the Columbia: The Story of a Migration." *The Beaver* (Spring 1971), 50–55. See also HBC archives for the article. Betts' article indicates that Chief Factor Duncan Finlayson had made arrangements for 23 families of settlers from the Red River Colony to move to the Columbia District, likely on Governor Simpson's orders.

[3] Geneva D. Lent, *West of the Mountains: James Sinclair and the Hudson's Bay Company* (Seattle: University of Washington Press, 1963), 80.

[4] John C. Jackson, *Children of the Fur Trade: Forgotten Metis of the Pacific Northwest* (Missoula: Montana Press, 1995), 94–95.

[5] Lent, *West of the Mountains*, 247. In response to the remarks about the racial inferiority of the Red River settlers, John Flett indignantly responded, "There were 17 families and but one Indian woman (Saskatchewan) among them." By this time some families of the original 23 had dropped out.

[6] Gail Morin, *Métis Families: A Genealogical Compendium* (Pawtacket, Rhode Island: Quinton, 1996).

[7] Lent, 57.

[8] Ibid., 42–45.

[9] Ibid., 103.

[10] Ibid., 100.

[11] Ibid., 109.

[12] Ibid., 109–110.

[13] Ibid., 111–112.

[14] The Blackfoot Confederacy included three powerful nations: the Blackfoot, the Blood and the Peigan. They had united to gain control of the vast buffalo plains of present day Saskatchewan and Alberta sometime before the Europeans arrived in the early 1700s. The three were independent nations but united by their Algonquian language and culture.

[15] Simpson's power extended over the HBC's vast North

Notes

American possessions which reached from the Hudson's Bay to the mouth of the Columbia River and from the American border to the Arctic Ocean.

[16] Sir George Simpson, Narrative of a Journey Round the World, Vol. II, 469.

[17] Simpson, *Narrative of a Journey Round the World, Vol. I,* 89. Simpson placed Saskatchewan's age at 75. Her burial record indicates she was 66.

[18] HBCA, A.36/6, Will of William Flett, 9 Nov. 1823.

[19] Simpson, 89.

[20] Jackson, *Children of the Fur Trade,* 201.

[21] Evidence suggests many Native midwives (*pamih*) attended Mixed-blood and Métis births.

[22] Simpson, 90.

[23] Ibid., 90–93.

CHAPTER 6
Journey into the Unknown

[1] William Flett Senior, age 30, and John Flett Senior, age 32, both came from Firth in the Orkney Islands. Both joined the HBC in 1782 (A.30/7, fo. 31). William Tomison in the *Saskatchewan Journals & Correspondence* speaks of them as brothers, 15 May, 1796. It is likely that William Flett Junior and John Flett Junior were cousins.

[2] John Flett, "Interesting Local History: A Sketch of the Emigration from Selkirk's Settlement to Pugent Sound in 1841," *Tacoma Daily Ledger,* 18 February 1885. Flett had previously published another version, "Oregon Reminiscences 1841" in the *Olympia Washington Standard,* 25 August, 1882. See John C. Jackson's *Children of the Fur Trade,* 293, n.172.

[3] William J. Betts, "From Red River to the Columbia." The article appeared in *The Beaver,* (Spring, 1971), 50–55, and is in the HBC Archives.

[4] Betts quoting John Flett, 53.

[5] The Anglicized version of the Cree, which has become more familiar when speaking of the famous chief is a phonetic compromise. The correct spelling of the Cree name varies.

What Lies Behind the Picture?

[6] Hugh A. Dempsey, "Maskepetoon," *Dictionary of Canadian Biography, Vol. IX* (Toronto, 1979), 537.
[7] Ibid.
[8] Ibid.
[9] Betts quoting John Flett, 53.
[10] Lent, *West of the Mountains*, 137.
[11] Betts quoting John Flett, 53–54. Some sources say that the party left their carts for horses at Fort Edmonton.
[12] Jackson, *Children of the Fur Trade*, 105. See also Simpson to Sinclair, 26 July 1841, HBCA, D.4/591, in Lent, 130.
[13] The only tribute to this remarkable journey is to James Sinclair who has Sinclair Pass and Sinclair Canyon named after him. Why Maski-pitoon was not so honoured is difficult to understand. In 1869 he entered a Blackfoot camp alone and unarmed, reportedly to negotiate peace. He was killed by Swan, a War Chief. See *Alberta History* (Spring 2002), Vol. 50, No. 2. 25. In 1957, Maskepetoon Park, a wildlife sanctuary near Red Deer, Alberta, was dedicated to the memory of the Cree peace-maker.
[14] See map of the journey on page 102 of John C. Jackson's *Children of the Fur Trade*.
[15] Lent, West of the Mountains, xii.
[16] Ibid., 156–58.
[17] Ibid., 164.
[18] Jackson, *Children of the Fur Trade*, 25.
[19] Ibid., 226.
[20] Ibid., 229.
[21] Ibid.
[22] Ibid., 248.
[23] D. N. Sprague and R. P. Fry, compilers: *The Genealogy of the First Metis Nation: The Development and Dispersal of the Red River Settlement 1820-1900* (Winnipeg: Pemmican Publications, 1983). Table 1 ID 1608 lists William Flett Junior and his wives Margaret McNab (1807–1838) and Mary Curtnir (1809–1854).
[24] HBCA, E.235/114.
[25] We are deeply indebted to Gordon C. Fielder and David G. Fielder, who are related to us through William Flett Senior and

Notes

Saskatchewan, for their tracing of their family tree, and the information they have found and shared with us about William Flett Junior and Saskatchewan.

[26]Lent, *West of the Mountains*, 161–62. Sinclair left the middle of December 1841 and wintered over in Fort Colville before returning to his family in the Red River Settlement by way of the Columbia River and Athabasca Pass. Maski-pitoon probably left in the autumn of 1841 to return to his people. It is likely that Saskatchewan journeyed with Sinclair to Fort Edmonton and then joined a party that was going to Red River.

[27]HBCA, E.4/2 fo. 145.

[28]The Indian Village became known as the Indian Settlement, or Swampy Settlement, or Saulteaux Settlement and latterly as St. Peter (Dynevor).

[29]Jackson, *Children of the Fur Trade*, 260. The actual boundary settlement was on 15 June 1846.

CHAPTER 7
Thomas Wishart: Adventure by Sea

[1]The Scots Ancestry Research Society of Edinburgh states, "The name Wishart is an ancient and distinguished one ... There is no mystery about the Wisharts reaching Orkney, because there was a fair amount of migration from Eastern Scotland (not least Angus) to Orkney, probably about the 15th and 16th centuries. No Wisharts seem to have become substantial landowners in Orkney."

[2]There were other Wisharts who came to Rupert's Land and the North West Territories. The Cumberland House Journal and Inland Journals in a footnote on page 218 states that Nicholas Wishart was from the Orkney Islands, signing on with the HBC as a tailor in 1776. Frequent references are made to him "making clothing for men." While stationed at Hudson House in 1784 he was "lost in the Barren grounds [the treeless Arctic plains west of Hudson Bay] and devoured by wolves." Edward Wishart was recruited from Orphir in Orkney in 1778 as a labourer. Frequent references are made to him in the Cumberland House Journal. James Wishart, age 35, was also

recruited from Orphir and served as Mate at York Factory 1814/15 B.239/d/166 fo. 445, 1M 683. George and James Wishart were brothers and served as seamen on board the HBC ship, *Morman Morison,* which carried immigrants to the new colony of Fort Victoria, Vancouver Island, in 1849. Another Wishart was the captain of the ship. Letters to the brothers from their family indicate they came from London. Their story of jumping ship was to turn into a tragedy for George, the Company, and the West Coast aboriginal people. Beattie and Buss, *Undelivered Letters* (Vancouver: University of British Columbia Press, 2003), 248–252.

[3] See Prince of Wales passenger list, 1819, 2M76, C. 1/78. Thomas Wishart, a labourer, age 23, embarked at Gravesend (near London), on May 22, 1819, and disembarked at York Factory on August 31. The source of many archival references are in Thomas Wishart bio-file, HBCA.

[4] John Franklin, *Narrative of a Journey to the Polar Sea in the Years 1819-20-21-22* (Vancouver: Douglas and MacIntyre, 2000), 17.

[5] Daniel Francis, *Discovery of the North* (Edmonton, 1986), 71–73

[6] Franklin, *Narrative,* 10–12.

[7] William P.L. Thomson, "Sober and Tractable," Rupert's Land Colloquium (Winnipeg, 1990), 3.

[8] Franklin, 31.

[9] Ibid., 32.

[10] Ibid., 34. Three hundred boats and twelve hundred men were engaged in 1819 in the service of the fishery.

[11] Ibid., 35.

[12] Pierre Berton, quoting John Ross. *The Arctic Grail: The Quest for the North West Passage and the Northern Pole* (Toronto: McClellan & Stewart, 1988), 27.

[13] Franklin, 36.

[14] Ibid., 37.

[15] Ibid., 38.

[16] George Back, *Arctic Artist: The Journal and Paintings of George Back, Midshipman with Franklin, 1819-22* (Montreal:

Notes

McGill-Queen's University Press, 1994), 4.
[17] Ibid., 4–5.
[18] Franklin, *Narrative*, 40.
[19] Ibid.
[20] Ibid.
[21] Back, *Arctic Artist*, 5.
[22] Two of the officers in Franklin's party, Hood and Back, were later to seek the affection of an Inuit woman. To prevent a duel for her hand, Franklin sent Back on an assignment. The woman had a child by Hood, who unfortunately was murdered when the party found themselves in dire circumstances.
[23] Franklin, *Narrative*, 40.

CHAPTER 8
Journey Inland

[1] Franklin, *Narrative*, 43.
[2] Ibid., 4.
[3] Lent, *West of the Mountains*, 35.
[4] Franklin, *Narrative*, 48–49.
[5] Ibid., 46.
[6] Ibid., 50.
[7] Ibid.
[8] Back, *Arctic Artist*, 17.
[9] Franklin, *Narrative*, 51.
[10] Ibid.
[11] Ibid., 51–52.
[12] Ibid.
[13] Norway House was located at what is now called Warren Landing on Big Mossey Point.
[14] Franklin, *Narrative*, 54.
[15] Daniel Francis, *Discovery of the North: The Exploration of Canada's Arctic* (Edmonton: Hurtig Publishers, 1986), 90, 97.
[16] Franklin, *Narrative*, 19.

CHAPTER 9
Thomas and Barbara

[1] W. L. Morton, *Manitoba: A History* (Toronto, 1957), 54.

What Lies Behind the Picture?

²Ibid. See Alexander Ross, *The Red River Settlement. Its Rise, Progress and Present State* (Edmonton: Hurtig Publishers, 1856 reprint, 1972) pp.135–143 in which he describes the terrible hardships the Selkirk settlers faced. He writes: "It is as if they had come to the Red River merely to endure its hardships, and as trusting pioneers to bear the heat and burden of the day, where a people of less hardihood and perseverance must necessarily have succumbed."

³J. M. Bumsted, *Fur Trade Wars* (Winnipeg: Great Plains Publication, 1999), 217.

⁴James G. MacGregor, *A History of Alberta,* 49ff.

⁵Bumsted, *Fur Trade Wars,* 234.

⁶Ross, *The Red River Settlement,* 50.

⁷Ibid., 56

⁸Bumsted, *Fur Trade Wars,* 49.

⁹Morton, *Manitoba,* 60.

¹⁰D.N. Sprague and R.P. Frye, compilers, *The Genealogy of the First Métis Nation:* Table 2: Family size, Personal property and Geographical Location of Landowners, 1835.

¹¹Bumsted, *Thomas Scott's Body* (Winnipeg: University of Manitoba Press, 2000), 80–81.

¹²Bumsted charts the six greatest floods from 1826 to 1950, page 89. See also "Red River Raging: The Flood of the Century," Manitoba, 1997, Video, Chronicled by CKND, Newsline: Copyright, CanWest Television Inc.).

¹³Morton, *Manitoba,* 66–67.

¹⁴Ibid.

¹⁵Shirley Wishart, *From the Red to the River of Many Rosebuds: Akokiniskway,* 2.

¹⁶In the Third Expedition by sea, 1845–47, Sir John Franklin and his entire party died of exposure and starvation. Thirty-nine expeditions searched for the Franklin party before its fate was finally determined. See Francis, *Discovery of the North,* 129–156.

¹⁷The 1840 Census, Iowa, records their residence in Clayton County. Thomas died in 1840. A copy of his probated will indicates that little was left to the family. The 1850 Census, Clayton

Notes

County, Iowa indicates that the family was dispersed. Thanks to relatives in the United States, we have been able to trace most of the family. Shirley, in her account of our ancestors, will pick up the story of the Wisharts in the United States.

CHAPTER 10
Eliza's Medicine Bag

[1] James Spence Jr.'s mother, Nestichio, was an English/Swampy Cree. His wife, Mary, was probably Assiniboine or Swampy Cree. See description of Swampy Cree in Chapter 1, n. 2. Some records indicate Mary was Métis or Mixed-Blood. Source of archival references to James Spence Jr. and Peter Flett, Eliza' father, are their bio-files, HBCA.

[2] Shirley Wishart, Personal correspondence with a relative.

[3] W. J. Healy, *Women of Red River* (Winnipeg: Russell Lang, 1923), 155–56.

[4] John J. Martin, *The Rosebud Trail*, 76.

[5] Donna G. Sutherland, personal correspondence, October 25, 2004.

[6] Terrance R. Anderson, "First Nations People and the Inculturation of the Gospel," *Touchstone,* Vol. 22, No. 1, January, 2004, 34.

[7] J. W. Grant, *Moon of Wintertime* (Toronto: University of Toronto Press, 1984), 73.

[8] Frits Pannekoek, *A Snug Little Flock* (Winnipeg: Watson & Dwyer, 1991), 80.

[9] Donna Sutherland, *Peguis: A Noble Friend* (Winnipeg: Derksen Printers, 2003), 89–115. Sutherland gives an account of the development of the Indian Settlement until it is firmly established.

[10] See also Annie L. Gaetz, *The Park Country: History of Red Deer and District* (Vancouver: Evergreen Press, 1948), 12.

[11] Jim Wishart had his name entered in Land Register B for lots 158, 159, 580 and 581, located at St. Paul's (Middlechurch). These lots, part of which Jim had under cultivation, part in woodlands, were on both sides of the Red River and comprised a total of 2,894 acres. See Wishart, *From the Red to the River of*

What Lies Behind the Picture?
Many Rosebuds, 4.
[12]Morton, *Manitoba,* 91, quoting A. K. Isbister, "The Hudson's Bay Territories," *Nor'Wester,* August 15, 1861.
[13]Sprague and Frye, Genealogy, Chart 5.
[14]For descriptions of the buffalo hunt see: Maria Campbell, *Riel's People: How the Métis Lived* (Vancouver: Douglas and MacIntyre, 1978), 16–18; Alexander Ross, *The Red River Settlement* (London, reprint 1856, Edmonton, 1952), 241–67. Father George Belcourt, "The Buffalo Hunt" *The Beaver* (December 1944).
[15]Morton, *Manitoba,* 85.
[16]Ibid., 85
[17]Ibid., 82ff.

CHAPTER 11
The Trek West and the Métis Struggle

[1]W. L. Morton, *Manitoba: A History,* 82–84.
[2]Ibid., 104.
[3]Ibid., 112–113.
[4]Ibid., 110–111.
[5]Ibid., 116–117.
[6]Ibid., 117.
[7]Ibid.
[8]Ibid.
[9]Bumsted, *Thomas Scott's Body,* 204. See also Bumsted, *Trials & Tribulations,* 189–213.
[10]Bumsted, *Thomas Scott's Body,* 197.
[11]Sarah Carter, *Aboriginal People and Colonizers of Western Canada to 1900* (Toronto: University of Toronto Press, 1999), 152.
[12]James' Orangeman regalia was stored in a trunk which was in the possession of the daughter of his youngest son, Herb. Unfortunately, the trunk and contents were destroyed by fire.
[13]Morton, *Manitoba,* 141ff.
[14]Correspondence between April 1873 to May 1900 indicates Jim's efforts to reclaim the land that was rightfully his. See Shirley Wishart, *From the Red to the River of Many Rosebuds,* 6.

Notes

[15] The High Bluff Methodist Circuit Register and Members' Roll show James and Eliza were received between 1878 and 1881 and that James was a steward. Source: Personal correspondence, Megan Kozminski, Archival Assistant, United Church Archives, Conference of Manitoba and Northwestern Ontario, May 12, 2004.

[16] Their friends were Rod and Ben McKenzie who farmed at Headingly, not far from Poplar Point. See Sprague and Frye, Table 5.

[17] James and Eliza had 13 children. Four were lost in childbirth or shortly after and their oldest, Barbara Ann, died when only 25. Those left behind in 1885 were Joseph James, age 27, George Robert, age 25, and their families, and Peter Henry, age 23, who was married in 1885.

[18] E.L. Meeres, *The Homesteads that Nurtured a City: The History of Red Deer, 1880-1905* (Red Deer: Fletcher Printing, 1977), 37.

[19] Ibid., 39.

[20] Ibid.

[21] Shirley Wishart, *The Long Bone Tunnel* (Calgary: Circle 5 Press, 1987).

[22] George Woodcock, *Gabriel Dumont* (Don Mills: Fitzhenry & Whiteside, 1978), 40.

[23] Carter, *Aboriginal People and Colonizers of Western Canada to 1900*, 154.

CHAPTER 12
Prairie Fires

[1] Annie L. Gaetz, *Park Country,* 22.

[2] Peter Erasmus, *Buffalo Days and Nights* (Calgary: Fifth House, 1999), 23.

[3] Personal correspondence between grandfather Dave Wishart and Shirley Wishart.

[4] Sarah Carter, *Aboriginal People and Colonizers,* 154.

[5] Hugh Dempsey, *Big Bear: The End of Freedom* (Vancouver: Greystone Books, 1984), 150.

[6] Joseph Kinsey Howard, *Strange Empire* (New York: William Morrow and Co., 1952), 379.

What Lies Behind the Picture?

[7] Ibid., 406. See also Blair Stonechild and Bill Waiser, *Loyal to Death: Indians and the North-West Rebellion* (Calgary: Fifth House, 1997), 79.

[8] Stonechild and Waiser, 29.

[9] Howard, *Strange Empire*, 392–93. See also George F.G. Stanley, *Louis Riel* (Toronto: McGraw-Hill Ryerson Limited, 1972), 318. Both give good accounts of the Duck Lake skirmish.

[10] Dempsey, *Big Bear*, 161. See also Howard, *Strange Empire*, 407–408 and D. W. Light, *Footprints in the Dust* (North Battleford: Turner-Warwick, 1987), 170 ff.

[11] Dempsey, 162–63, gives possible reasons for the massacre. See also his description of the fate of the nine bodies in Chapter 11, n.1. See also footnote 27 in Chapter 9 page 213 for the number of inconsistencies in the various accounts of the massacre.

[12] Gaetz, *Park Country*, 21. The hostile Natives may have been the Cree from the Battle River area. Under Chief Bobtail, and spurred on by starvation and privation, they began pillaging and attacking wagon trains. A full-scale uprising was prevented when Captain John Ostell of the Alberta Field Force reached the Battle River Crossing on April 28.

[13] Ibid.

[14] Ibid., 21–22.

[15] Ibid.

[16] Gaetz., 22–24.

[17] Ibid., 24.

[18] Ibid., 24–25.

[19] The Blackfoot Confederacy as mentioned earlier was made up of Blood, Blackfoot and Piegan. Some sources include Sarcee and Stony.

[20] Stonechild and Waiser, *Loyal to Death*, 178.

[21] Bob Beal and Rod Macleod, *Prairie Fire: The 1885 North-West Rebellion.* (Edmonton: Hurtig Publishers, 1984), 208ff.

[22] Stonechild and Waiser, *Loyal to Death*, 175.

[23] Beal and Macleod, *Prairie Fire*, 209.

[24] Ibid.

[25] Stonechild and Waiser, *Loyal to Death*, 175.

Notes

[26] Gaetz, *Park Country,* 25.
[27] Ibid., 25–26.
[28] Ibid., 26.
[29] Ibid., 26–27.
[30] Ibid.
[31] Ibid.

CHAPTER 13
The Aftermath of the Rebellion

[1] Beal and Macleod, *Prairie Fire,* 276.
[2] Howard, *Strange Empire,* 549.
[3] Ibid., 560–62
[4] Meeres, *The Homesteads...,* 39. Pine Lake is east of Innisfail, Alberta.
[5] Howard, See Introduction by Nicholas C.P. Vrooman, xxi-xxii.
[6] Petersen and Brown, *The New Peoples* (Winnipeg: University of Manitoba Press, 1953), 4. See also Mike Brodgens, "The Rise and Fall of Western Métis in the Criminal Justice Process" in *Struggle for Recognition: Canadian Justice and the Métis Nations,* (Winnipeg: Pemmican Publications, 1991), 39–51. Brogens attempts to prove that the Métis were purposely marginalized and kept in their place by the criminal justice system and used as cheap labour for agriculture in the Canadian West. See also Murray Dobbin who documents the hopelessness and despair of the Alberta and Saskatchewan Métis after 1885 in *The One-and-a-Half Men,* (Regina: Gabriel Institute of Native Studies and Applied Research, 1981). See also Jean Goodwill and Norma Sluman in *John Tootoosis* (Winnipeg: Pemmican, 1984), 76. They describe how all the Indian reserves and Métis settlements considered to be involved in any way in the North West Rebellion were searched for any prominent rebels remaining at large. In the process they were looted and anything of value was taken: furs, horses, as well as souvenirs—beadwork, drums, rattles, headgear....
[7] Carter, *Aboriginal People...,* 157–159.
[8] Ibid., 161.

What Lies Behind the Picture?

[9] Ibid., 162.
[10] Ibid.
[11] Ibid., 163–164.
[12] Ibid., 168–169.
[13] Ibid.
[14] A "Permit" system for selling produce was instituted on reserves in 1881. A permit was necessary to sell logs, a horse, a cow—it was forbidden to kill a cow to feed one's family unless one had a permit. A permit was required to sell produce and the recipient was required to declare that "I paid the above Indian for the article described the sum of ___. Please insert the amount paid, sign and return the original permit by bearer." This law, although not actively enforced in later years (1950s onward) was not officially revoked until 1995. Copies of such permits can be seen in the Allen Sapp Gallery (The Gonor Collection in North Battleford, Saskatchewan). See also Joseph F. Dion, *My Tribe the Crees* (Calgary: Glenbow, 1979), 132–33.
[15] Carter, Aboriginal People, 169.
[16] Harold Cardinal, *The Unjust Society* (Vancouver: Douglas & MacIntyre, 1969), 12.
[17] Thomas King, *The Truth About Stories: A Native Narrative* (Toronto: Anansi Press, 2003), 132–133.
[18] Carter, 150.

CHAPTER 14
Journey to the Promised Land

[1] John J. Martin, *The Rosebud Trail,* 1962, 74.
[2] See Carter's discussion in *Aboriginal People and the Colonizers of Western Canada to 1900,* 156–57.
[3] Howard, *Strange Empire,* xxi.
[4] For a description of High Eagle, the geography and Native lore surrounding Rosebud, see Shirley Wishart, citing the late John J. Martin in *From the Red to the River of Many Rosebuds: Akokiniskway,* 1–8.
[5] The particular place they settled in the Rosebud valley became known as Redland.

Notes

CHAPTER 15
They Are Remembered

[1] Kerry Wood, Chapter 1, "The Setting" in *The Sanctuary,* (Edmonton, 1952) 11–16.

[2] William Flett, in addition to his duties as Master and Canoe man, was placed in charge of Edmonton House (Fort Edmonton) from May to September, 1819, as well as on other occasions.

[3] The Heritage Centre is located in the Prince of Wales Armories, Edmonton, Alberta.

CHAPTER 16
My Personal Journey

[1] I was a delegate to the 31st General Council of the United Church of Canada held in Sudbury, Ontario, August, 1986 when an apology to First Nations Peoples was made. It stated:

Long before my people journeyed to this land your people were here and you received from your Elders an understanding of creation and of the Mystery that surrounds us all that was deep, and rich, and to be treasured. We did not hear you when you shared your vision. In our zeal to tell you the good news of Jesus Christ we were closed to the value of your spirituality.

We confused Western ways and culture with the depth and breadth and length and height of the gospel of Christ. We imposed our civilization as a condition of accepting the gospel. We tried to make you like us and in doing so we helped destroy the vision that made you what you were. As a result, you, and we, are poorer and the image of the Creator in us is twisted, blurred, and we are not what we are meant by God to be. We ask you to forgive us and to walk together with us in the Spirit of Christ so that our peoples may be blessed and God's creation healed.

[2] Martin, *The Rosebud Trail,* 77.

[3] Ibid.

[4] Wishart, *From the Red to the River of Many Rosebuds, Akokiniskway,* 4.

[5] Ibid., 5

What Lies Behind the Picture?

⁶Virginia Barter, "Searching for the Silver Fox: A Fur Trade Family History." *The Rupert's Land Newsletter,* The Centre for Rupert's Land Studies at the University of Winnipeg, No. 18 (Spring 2005), 7–8.

⁷Pierre Berton, *The Joy of Writing* (Toronto: Doubleday, 2003), 34.

EPILOGUE
Defining Moments

¹Holy Bible, "The Revelation to John" Chapter 21: 4.

Bibliography

PRIMARY SOURCES

Hudson's Bay Company Archives, Archives of Manitoba, Winnipeg.
Provincial Archives of Alberta, Edmonton.
Bio-file, James Spence, Sr. (HBCA)
Bio-file, James Spence, Jr. (HBCA)
Bio-file, William Flett, Sr. (HBCA)
Bio-file, Thomas Wishart (HBCA)
Bio-file, Peter Flett (HBCA)

PRIMARY PUBLISHED SOURCES

Glover, Richard ed. *Samuel Hearne: A Journey from Prince of Wales Fort in Hudson's Bay to the Northern Ocean (1795).* Toronto: MacMillan, 1958.

Johnson, Alice M., ed. *Saskatchewan Journals and Correspondence: Edmonton House 1795-1800, Chesterfield House 1800-1802.* London: The Hudson's Bay Record Society, XXVI, 1967.

Nicks, John, "The Diary of a Young Fur Trader: The 1789–1790 Journal of Thomas Staynor," in Lewis H. Thomas, ed., *Essays*

The Story Behind the Picture

in Western History in Honour of Lewis Gwynne Thomas. Edmonton: University of Alberta Press, 1976.

Rich, E. E. & A. M. Johnson, eds. *Cumberland House Journal and Inland Journals 1775-82 First Series, and Second Series, 1779-82.* London: The Hudson's Bay Record Society, XIV (1951) and XV (1952).

The Publications of the Hudson's Bay Company Record Society: Hudson's Bay Company 1670-1870, Vol. 2 1763-1870, (London).

Tyrrel, J. B., ed. *Journals of Samuel Hearne & Philip Turnor, 1774-1792.* Toronto: Champlain Society, 1934.

SECONDARY PUBLISHED SOURCES

Adams, John. *Old Square-Toes and His Lady.* Victoria: Horsdal & Shubert, 2001.

Anderson, Terence R. "First Nations People and the Inculturation of the Gospel," *Touchstone,* Vol 22, January 2004: Number 1.

Armstrong, G. H. *The Origin and Meaning of Place Names in Canada.* Toronto: MacMillan of Canada, 1972.

Back, George. *Arctic Artist: The Journal and Paintings of George Back, Midshipman with Franklin, 1819-1822.* Montreal: McGill-Queen's University Press, 1994.

Barter, Virginia. "Searching for the Silver Fox: A Fur Trade Family History," *The Rupert's Land Newsletter,* The Centre for Rupert's Land Studies at the University of Winnipeg, No. 18 (Spring 2005).

Beal, Bob & Macleod, Rod. *Prairie Fire: The 1885 North West Rebellion.* Edmonton: Hurtig Publishers, 1984.

Beattie, Judith Hudson Beattie, and Buss, Helen M. eds. *Undelivered Letters to Hudson's Bay Company Men on the Northwest Coast of America, 1830-57.* Vancouver: University of British Columbia Press, 2003.

Berton, Pierre. *The Arctic Grail: The Quest for the North West Passage.* Toronto: McClellan & Stewart, 1988.

_____ *The Joy of Writing.* Toronto: Doubleday Canada, 2003.

Binnema, Theodore; Ens, Gerhard J. & R. C. Macleod., eds.

Bibliography

From Rupert's Land to Canada. Edmonton: University of Alberta Press, 2001.

Brown, Jennifer S. H. *Strangers in Blood: Fur Trade Company Families in Indian Country.* Vancouver: University of British Columbia Press, 1985.

_____ "Isaac Batt", *Dictionary of Canadian Biography, Vol. IV, 1771-1800.* Toronto: University of Toronto Press, 1979.

Bumsted, J. M. *Fur Trade Wars: The Founding of Western Canada.* Winnipeg: Great Plains Publications, 1999.

_____ *Thomas Scott's Body: and Other Essays on Early Manitoba History.* Winnipeg: University of Manitoba Press, 2000.

_____ *Trials & Tribulations: The Red River Settlement and the Emergence of Manitoba 1811-1870.* Winnipeg: Great Plains Publication, 2003.

Campbell, Maria. *Riel's People: How they Lived.* Vancouver: Douglas & MacIntyre, 1978.

Canadian Broadcasting Corporation, Television Series: *Canada: A People's History,* Episode 10, "Taking the West," 2001.

Carbyn, Lu. *The Buffalo Wolf: Predators, Prey and the Politics of Nature.* Washington: Smithsonian Institute, 2003.

Cardinal, Harold. *The Unjust Society.* Vancouver/Toronto: Douglas & McIntyre, 1969. Published simultaneously in the United States by The University of Washington Press, Seattle.

Carter, Sarah. *Aboriginal People and Colonizers of Western Canada to 1900.* Toronto: University of Toronto Press, 1999.

Dempsey, Hugh A. "Maskepetoon (Broken Arm, Crooked Arm, baptized Abraham)" *Dictionary of Canadian Biography, Vol IX, 1861-70,* pp. 537–38. Toronto: University of Toronto Press, 1979.

_____ *Big Bear: The End Of Freedom.* Vancouver: Greystone Books, 1984.

Dickason, Olive Patricia. *Canada's First Nations: A History of Founding Peoples from Earliest Times.* Toronto: McLelland & Stewart Inc., 1992.

_____ "One Nation in its North East to New Nation in the North West: A Look at the Emergence of the Métis." *The*

What Lies Behind the Picture?

New Peoples: Being and Becoming in North America. Peterson & Brown eds. Winnipeg: University of Manitoba Press, 1985.

Dion, Joseph F. *My Tribe the Crees* (Edited and with an Introduction by Hugh A. Dempsey). Calgary: Glenbow, 1979.

Dobbin, Murray. *The One-and-a-Half Men: The Story of Jim Brady & Malcolm Norris Métis Patriots of the 20th Century*. Regina: Gabriel Dumont Institute of Native Studies and Applied Research, 1981.

Erasmus, Peter (As told to Henry Thompson). *Buffalo Days And Nights*. Calgary: Fifth House Ltd., 1999

Francis, Daniel. *Discovery of the North: The Exploration of Canada's Arctic*. Edmonton: Hurtig Publishers, 1986

Franklin, John. *Narrative of a Second Expedition to the Shores of the Polar Sea in the years 1825, 1826 & 1827*. Edmonton: M.G. Hurtig Ltd, 1971.

_____*Narrative of a Journey to the Polar Sea in the years 1819-20-21-22*. Vancouver: Douglas & McIntyre, 2000.

Friesen, John W. *The Riel/Real Story: An Interpretive History of the People of Canada*. Ottawa: Borealis Press, 1996.

Gaetz, Annie L. *The Park Country: History of Red Deer (Alberta) and District*. Vancouver: Evergreen Press Ltd, 1948. Revised 1960.

Goodwill, Jean and Sluman, Norma. *John Tootoosis*. Winnipeg: Pemmican Publications Inc., 1984.

Grant, John Webster. *Moon of Wintertime: Missionaries and the Indians of Canada in Encounter since 1534*. Toronto: University of Toronto Press, 1984.

Groves, Naomi Jackson. *A.Y.'S Canada*. Toronto/Vancouver: Clarke, Irwin & Company Limited, 1968.

Hawker, Peter D. *Fort Edmonton: Fur Trade Entrepôt 1795-1870*. Edmonton: A Hawk Production, 1995.

Healy, W. J. *Women of Red River*. Winnipeg: Russell Lang, 1923.

Howard, Joseph Kinsey. *Strange Empire: A Narrative of the Northwest*. New York: William Morrow & Company, 1952. (New material copyright by the Minnesota Historical Society, 1970).

Bibliography

Huck, Barbara et al. *Exploring Fur Trade Routes of North America.* Winnipeg: Heartland, 2002.

Hymas, Kay, ed. *Akokiniskway "by the river of many roses."* Rosebud: printed by The Rosebud Historical Society, 1983.

Jackson, John C. *Children of the Fur Trade: Forgotten Métis of the Pacific Northwest.* Missoula, Montana: Mountain Press, 1995.

_____ *Jemmy Jock Bird: Marginal Man on the Blackfoot Frontier.* Calgary: University of Calgary Press, 2003.

Jenkins, Philip. *Dream Catchers: How Mainstream America Discovered Native Spirituality.* New York: Oxford University Press, 2004.

Johnson, Dennis F. *Inland Armada: The York Boats of the Hudson's Bay Company.* Manitoba: Lower Fort Garry Volunteer Association Inc. Selkirk, 2005.

King, Thomas. *The Truth About Stories: A Native Narrative.* The Massey Lecture Series 2003. Toronto: Anansi Press, 2003.

Lake–Thom, Bobby. *Spirits of the Earth: A Guide to Native American Nature Symbols, Stories and Ceremonies.* New York: Plume (Penguin Books), 1997

Lent, D. Geneva. *West of the Mountains: James Sinclair and the Hudson's Bay Company.* Seattle: University of Washington Press, 1963.

Light, Douglas W. *Footprints in the Dust.* North Battleford: Turner-Warwick Publications Inc., 1987.

MacGregor, James G. *A History of Alberta.* Edmonton: Hurtig Publishers, 1972.

Marsh, James. "Samuel Hearne" *The Canadian Encyclopedia, Vol 2.* Edmonton: Hurtig Publishers, 1985.

Martin, John J. *The Rosebud Trail.* (Self-Published, 1962).

MacDonald, George Heath. *Fort-Augustus-Edmonton: Northwest Trails and Traffic.* Edmonton: Douglas Print Co., 1954.

Meeres, E.L. *The Homesteads that Nurtured A City: The History of Red Deer, 1880-1905.* Red Deer:Fletcher Printing, 1977.

Melnycky, Peter, "Spence of Buckingham House: A Case Study of Genealogy and Fur Trade Biography". *Rupert's Land*

What Lies Behind the Picture?

Colloquium Papers. Edmonton 1994: Published by Centre for Rupert's Land Studies, Winnipeg 1994.
Morton, W. L. *Manitoba: A History.* Toronto: University of Toronto Press, 1957.
Morin, Gail. *Métis Families: A Genealogical Compendium.* Pawtacket, Rhode Island: Quinton, 1996.
↙Newman, Peter C. *Company of Adventures.* Markham: Viking Penguin Publishing Ltd., 1985.
_____*Empire of the Bay.* Toronto: Madison Press Books, 1989.
Nisbet, Jack. *Sources of the River: Tracking David Thompson Across Western North America.* Seattle: Sasquatch Books, 1994.
Pannekoek, Frits. *A Snug Little Flock: The Social Origins of the Riel Resistance of 1869-1870.* Winnipeg: Watson & Dwyer Publishing Ltd., 1991.
Peterson, Jacqueline and Brown, Jennifer S. H. eds. *The New Peoples: Being and Becoming Metis in North America.* Winnipeg: University of Manitoba Press, 1985.
Ream, Peter T. *The Fort on the Saskatchewan.* Edmonton: Metropolitan Printing, 1974.
Rodriguez, Richard. Brown: *The Last Discovery of America.* New York: Viking, 2002.
Ross, Alexander. *The Red River Settlement: Its Rise, Progress, and Present State.* Edmonton: Hurtig Publishers (Reprint of 1856 edition), 1972.
Simpson, Sir George. *Narrative of a Journey Round the World: During the years 1841-42, Vol I & II.* London: Henry Colburn Publisher, 1841.
Sprague, D. N. and Frye, R. P., compilers. *The Genealogy of the First Nation: The Development and Dispersal of the Red River Settlement 1820-1900.* Two Volumes. Winnipeg: Pemmican Publications, 1983.
Stanley, G. F. G. *Louis Riel, Patriot or Rebel?* Ottawa: The Canadian Historical Associaton, No. 2, 1964.
Stenson, Fred. *The Trade.* Vancouver: Douglas & McIntyre, 1978.
Stonechild, Blair & Waiser, Bill. *Loyal Till Death: Indians and the North-West Rebellion.* Calgary: Fifth House Ltd., 1997.

Bibliography

Sutherland, Donna G. *Peguis: A Noble Friend.* Winnipeg: Derksen Printers Ltd., 2003.

Thomson, William P. L. "Sober and Tractable? The Hudson's Bay Men in their Orkney Context." *Rupert's Land Colloquium Papers: Stromness 1990,* Published by Centre for Rupert's Land Studies, Winnipeg: 1990.

Thorson, Bruce. "The Bay Connection: Orkney Islanders Discover their Métis heritage." *Canadian Geographic,* (November/December), Ottawa: 2000.

Van Kirk, Sylvia. *"Many Tender Ties": Women in Fur Trade Society, 1670-1870.* Winnipeg: Watson & Dwyer Publishing Ltd., 1980 (fifth printing 1993).

_____ "Tracing the Fortunes of Five Founding Families of Victoria." *British Columbia Studies,* No. 115 & 116 (Autumn/Winter 1997/98).

Wilson, Clifford. "Anthony Henday," *Dictionary of Canadian Biography* Volume III, 1740 to 1770, pp. 285–287. Toronto: University of Toronto Press, 1974.

Wishart, D. J. *An Unspeakable Sadness: The Dispossession of the Nebraska Indian.* Lincoln: University of Nebraska Press, 1997.

Wishart, Shirley Aulta. *From the Red to the River of Many Rosebuds: Akokiniskway.* Calgary: Self-published by Shirley Wishart, 1983.

_____ "Circles Within Circles: The Linkage of Hudson's Bay Company Fur Trade Families in Rupert's Land." *Rupert's Land Colloquium Papers,* Edmonton: 1994, edited by Ian MacLaren, Michael Payne and Heather Rollason. Published by Centre for Rupert's Land Studies, Winnipeg: 1994.

_____ "Telling the Ancestors," *Rupert's Land Newsletter,* No. 5 (Fall.) Centre for Rupert's Land Studies, Winnipeg: 1998.

Wolfart, H. C. & Ahenakew, Freda. *They Knew Both Sides of Medicine: Cree Tales of Curing and Cursing Told by Alice Ahenakew.* Winnipeg: The University of Manitoba Press, 2000.

Wood, Kerry. *The Sanctuary.* Edmonton: Hamly Press Ltd., 1952.

Woodcock, George. *Gabriel Dumont: The Canadians.* Don Mills: Fitzhenry & Whiteside Ltd., 1978.

Index

Page numbers in **bold** refer to illustrations, photographs, and maps.

Acheson, Bill, 179–80, 184
Acton House, 72, 74

Back, George, 105
Baergen, Bill, 185
Ballard, Mary, 185
Barter, Virginia, 178
Batoche, Saskatchewan, 144, 147, 155–56, 161–62
Batt, Isaac (1731–1791)
  cultural heritage honours, 169
  as HBC employee, 30–41, 44
  wives and family, 30, 35–37, 39–41
Batt, James (Isaac's brother, Nestichio's uncle), 45–46, 57
Batt, Nestichio (1757–1827, Isaac's daughter, James Spence's wife)
  children of, 50–53
  cultural heritage honours, 169
  early life, 35, 42
  life as Spence's wife, 44–52, 57
Battle of Seven Oaks, 114
Battleford, Saskatchewan, 147
Beal, Bob, 155
bears, 36
beavers and beaver skins, 32, 37, 46–47, 108–9

219

What Lies Behind the Picture?

Big Bear, 148–49
Bird, James, Jr., 73
Blackfoot people
  Confederacy, 81, 196n14, 206n19
  and HBC, 33, 59
  name for Rosebud area, 161
  NW Rebellion of 1885 and, 152–59
  relations with Cree people, 86, 88, 93, 147
  See also Native people
Blizzard of 1887, Great. *See* Great Blizzard of 1887
boats. *See* river travel
Buckingham House, 48–51, 58, 169
buffalo and buffalo hunts, 64, **64,** 84, 88, 121, 130, 133, 134, 147, 194n20–21
Bumsted, Thomas, 159

Calgary. *See* Fort Calgary
California gold rush, 97
canoes, 44, **45,** 67, 133
Cardinal, Harold, 158, 176
Carter, Sarah, 157, 158
Catholicism, Roman, 96, 138, 146
Central Alberta Historical Society, 179
Clayton County, Iowa, 122, 185, 203n17
Cockran, Rev. William, Red River Settlement, 128–29

Colen, Joseph, York Factory, 46
Cook, Mary (daughter of James and Eliza Wishart), 16
Cowlitz Farm, British Columbia, 78, **94**
Crane, Louise, 177
Crane Bear (Blackfoot), 16
Cree people
  Beaver Hill Cree, 72–73
  Cree language, 60–61
  marriage customs, 36–37, 61–63, 65
  NW Rebellion of 1885 and, 147–59
  relations with Blackfoot people, 86, 88, 93, 147
  See also Native people
Cree woman (1740–1792, Isaac Batt's wife, unknown name), 30, 35–37, 41
Crowfoot, Chief, 147, 152
Crozier, L.N.F., 148
Cumberland House, Manitoba, 38, 44, 112, 199n2
  map of York Factory to, 111
Curtnir, Mary (wife of William Flett, Jr.), 97

Dawe, Mary, 184
Dawe, Michael, 164, 184
Delaney, Theresa, 148
Denney, Charles, 178, 183
Duck Lake, Saskatchewan, 147–49, 152

Index

Dumont, Gabriel, 140, 148, 155

Edmonton House
daily life at, 69–75
founding of (1795), 57–59
See also Fort Edmonton;
Hudson's Bay Company

"Eliza's Lament" (poem), 143–44

Elk Point Heritage Centre, 169

Fargey, Jim, 184
Farrell, Sharyl, 185
Fidler, Peter, 49, 57–59, 170, 176
Fielder, Gordon C. and David G., 184
Finlay, Cam, 184
Flett, Eliza. *See* Wishart, Eliza Flett (1835–1900, James' wife, Vern's great-grandmother)
Flett, Euphemia Halcro. *See* Halcro, Euphemia (1816–1907, Peter Flett's wife)
Flett, John, 86–89, 96–97
Flett, Peter (1811–unknown, son of William Flett and Saskatchewan), 70–72, 126, 129
Flett, William, Jr., and children, 77–78, 87, 97
Flett, William, Sr. (1762–1823, Saskatchewan's husband), 71

children of, 68, 74–75, 77–78, 87
cultural heritage honours, 169–70
death and burial, 74, 98
at Edmonton House, 69–75
as HBC employee, 45, 56–75, 87
with Saskatchewan, 60–76
Fort Augustus (NWC), 59
Fort Calgary, 145–46
NW Rebellion of 1885 and, 150–54
Fort Carlton, 60, 80, 82
Fort Colville, 97
Fort Douglas, 52
Fort Edmonton, 88, 90–91
mail service to Calgary, 145–46
NW Rebellion of 1885 and, 152–55
Oregon Territory colonists at, 80, 82, 86–88
See also Edmonton House
Fort Ellice, 80
Fort Enterprise, 113
Fort Garry, 82, 177
Fort George (NWC), 48, 169
Fort Gibralter (NWC), 52
Fort Macleod, 89, 153
Fort Nisqually, 78, 94, 95
Fort Pitt, 80, 86, 147
Fort Vancouver and area, 78, 93–96, 94
Fowler, Sarah (Isaac Batt's

What Lies Behind the Picture?

English wife), 35
Franklin, John, 102–13, 201n22, 202n16
Frobisher, Thomas, 39
Frog Lake massacre, 148–49, 152, 157
fur trade era
   articles for trading, 46–48, 108–9
   beavers and beaver skins, 32, 37, 46–47, 108–9
   daily life in, 45–48, 65–66, 69–70, 74–75
   French traders in, 32–34, 37
   literacy skills for, 45–46
   lost child incident, 71–72
   racism, 74–75
   See also Hudson's Bay Company; marriage customs; North West Company; Oregon Territory colonists; river travel

Gaetz, Annie, Red Deer, 150, 183
Gaetz, John L. (Jack), Red Deer, 160, 164–67, **166**
Gaetz, Ray, Red Deer, 150
Gaetz Lake Sanctuary, Red Deer, 22, 164, 167
genealogical chart, 24–25
Gleichen, 16, 21, 142, 162
Gowanlock, Theresa, 148
Graham, Andrew (Chief Factor), 38
grain elevators, 15
Grant, John Webster, 128
Great Blizzard of 1887, 16–20
Gros Ventre people, 40, 59

Halcro, Euphemia (1816–1907, Peter Flett's wife), 126, 129
Half-breed
   as term, 20
   See also North-West Rebellion of 1885; racism; Red River Resistance of 1870; Red River Settlement
HBC. *See* Hudson's Bay Company
Hearne, Samuel, 36–38
Henday, Anthony, 33–34, 36
Henry, Alexander, 39
Hepburn, Don, 185
Herman, Judy, 180
Heron, Francis, 69–70, 73–74
Hertfordshire, England, 30
High Eagle (Blackfoot), 162, 208n4
Hill's Gates Portage, 110–12
Howard, Joseph Kinsey, 156
Hudson House, 44, 199n2
Hudson's Bay Company, 60
   archives, 185
   disposition of employees' estates, 50–52, 74
   early history of, 32–35, 45–46
   first murder of an HBC employee by Natives, 40

Index

NWC amalgamation with, 114–17
NWC relations, 37–39, 46–48, 52, 59, 73–74
Orcadian employees, 42–43, 45–46, 48, 56–57, 102–3
salaries and wages, 195n4
See also Edmonton House; Fort Edmonton; fur trade era; maps; Oregon Territory colonists; Simpson, George (HBC Governor); York Factory (HBC)
Indian Act, 157–58
Indian Settlement. *See* St. Peter's Parish, Red River Settlement
Indians. *See* Native people
Inuit people, 105–6
Iowa, Wishart family in, 122, 185, 203n17
Isaac's House, Saskatchewan, 39
Isbister, A.K., 130
Isham, James, 33–34

Jacobson, Jolene, 180
Jasper House, 92, 98
Jock, Jemmy, 46

Kenney, David, Rosebud, 167, 184
King, Thomas, 158

Lacombe, Father, 152, 154
Lennie, Tom and Mary, Red Deer area, 145, 150–51
Logan, Robert, Selkirk colony, 117
Low, George, Orcadian, 42–43

MacKenzie, Beth (Vern's daughter), 185
Macleod, Rod, 155
Manchester House, Saskatchewan, 40, 44, 49–50
Manitoba Act of 1870, 138
maps
  Hudson's Bay Company posts (1832), 10–11
  Orkney, Scotland, 43
  Red River Settlement and area, 118–19
  route of Oregon Territory colonists, 94–95
  Rupert's Land (after 1818), 28–29
  Saskatchewan River country, 149
  York Factory to Cumberland House, 111
  York Factory to Red River, 116
marriage customs
  burials and estates, 50–52, 74, 98
  country marriages, 34–37, 44, 50–51, 61–63, 74–75, 195n6

223

What Lies Behind the Picture?

English wives, 35, 74–75
HBC and NWC policies,
   34–37, 50–51, 61, 65
Native customs, 36–37,
   61–62, 65
Marten, Henry (Chief
   Factor), 41
Martin, Humphrey (Chief
   Factor), 39, 56
Martin, John, Rosebud, 15–16,
   126–27, 183
Maski-pitoon, Chief (Cree),
   87–88, 92–93, 198n13, 199n26
McDougall, Rev. John, 154
McGillivray, Duncan, 59
McKenzie, Rod and Ben, Red
   Deer area, 140, 142, 205n16
McNabb, Margaret (wife of
   William Flett, Jr.), 77
Meeres, E.L., 141–42
Melnycky, Peter, 183–84
Métis
   as term, 20
   See also North-West
      Rebellion of 1885; racism;
      Red River Resistance of
      1870; Red River Settlement
missionaries, Christian,
   87–88, 128–30, **129**, **131**
Mixed-blood
   as term, 20
   See also North-West
      Rebellion of 1885; racism;
      Red River Resistance of
      1870; Red River Settlement

moose, 47
Mortensen, Dianna, 185
Munro, Hugh, 70–71

Native people, 31
   NW Rebellion of 1885 and,
      147–59
   racism and, 74–75, 157–58
   reserves, permits, and pass-
      es, 157–59, 208n14
   spirituality and healing,
      127–28, 186n8
   terminology for, 20
   United Church apology to,
      209n1
   views of bears, 36
   women's skills, 49, 70
   See also Blackfoot people;
      Cree people; racism
Nestichio Batt. See Batt,
   Nestichio (1757–1827, Isaac's
   daughter, James Spence's
   wife)
North West Company
   HBC amalgamation with,
      114–17
   HBC relations with, 37–39,
      41, 46–48, 52, 59, 72–74
   marriage customs and poli-
      cies, 61, 65
   See also fur trade era
North West Mounted Police,
   153
North-West Rebellion of 1885
   events of, 144, 147–57

Index

impact on Métis after, 157–59, 207n6
Norton, Moses (HBC Chief Factor), 37
Norway House, 112
NWC. *See* North West Company

Orangeman, 138
Oregon Territory colonists
  agreement with U.S., 77
  journey to Fort Edmonton, 77–91
  journey from Edmonton to Fort Vancouver, 92–95
  life in Oregon Territory, 95–99
  map of route of colonists, 94–95
Orkney, Scotland, 43
  boat-building skills, 67
  HBC employees from, 42–46, 48, 56–57, 102–3
  literacy of workers, 45
  Wisharts in, 199n1
Oxford House, 110

Paris, Peter, 176
Parry, William Edward, 103
Payne, Michael, 183–84
pedlars, fur trade. *See* North West Company
Peguis (Saulteaux), 129
pemmican, 126, 130–31
Poplar Point Parish, Red River Settlement, 130, 139
portage, 66–67, **67**, 110–12
Porter, Lois, 184
Poundmaker, 147–48

racism
  impact on Vern Wishart's family, 13–16, 20–23, 172–82
  missionaries and, 128–29
  in Oregon Territory, 95–97
  in Red River settlement, 74–75, 96, 98
  self-identification and, 9
  terminology and, 20–21
  United Church apology to Native people (1986), 209n1
  and westward expansion, 135–36
Red Deer Crossing and area
  life in, 89, 140–46, **141**
  NW Rebellion of 1885 and, 149–59
Red River carts, 78–81, **79**, **81**, 89, 133
Red River floods, 120–21, 202n12
Red River Resistance of 1870, 134–39
Red River Settlement
  daily life in, 124–33
  history of, 51–52, 74–75, 114–21, 124–26
  maps of, **116**, 118–19
  missionaries in, 128–30, **129**

225

What Lies Behind the Picture?

Oregon Territory colonists from, 77–78, 82–85
Redland, 208n5
Reed, Hayter, 157, 158
Riel, Louis
Red River Resistance of 1870 and, 136–40, **137**, 144, 161
NW Rebellion of 1885 and, 146–48, 155–56, 161
river travel
canoes, 44, **45**, 67
in fur trade era, 65–70, **67**, 109–13, 133
steersmen, 44, 50, 65
York boats, 44, **57**, 65–67, 73, 87
Roemmich, Carolina, 184
Roman Catholicism, 96, 138, 146
Rosebud area, 15–16, 160–62, 167–69, **168**
See also Great Blizzard of 1887
Ross, John, explorer, 104
Rowand, John, 85, 87
Rowand, John, Jr., wife (Margaret Harriet) and child, **63**
Rowland, Robert and Elizabeth, 76
Rundle, Robert T., 87
Rupert's Land
history of, 32, 135–36
map of (1818), **28–29**

Saskatchewan (1775–1845, Cree, William Flett's wife), 60–99
children and grandchildren of, 68, 74–75, 77–78, 97, 129
cultural heritage honours, 169
at Edmonton House, 69–75
as Oregon Territory colonist, 76–79, 82–85, 97
return to Red River area, 97–98, **99**
as wife of William Flett, 60–75
Saskatchewan River area (map), **149**
Saulteaux, 129
Scotland. See Orkney, Scotland
Selkirk, Lord (Thomas Douglas), 51–52
Selkirk colony
during HBC/NWC amalgamation, 114–17
map of York Factory to, **116**
Simpson, George (HBC Governor)
during amalgamation with NWC, 115–18
as Governor of HBC, 60, 73, 76–78, 82, **83**
and Oregon Territory colonists, 82–85, 92, 184
Sinclair, James
cultural heritage honours, 198n13

Index

as Oregon Territory colonist, 78–80, 88–94
return to Red River settlement, 97–98
Spence, Barbara (1800–1904, wife of Thomas Wishart)
children of, 118–22, 124
in Iowa, 122, 185, 203n17
in Red River area, 117–22
Spence, Clifford, Brentwood Bay, B.C., 189n28, 192n26
Spence, James, Jr. (1781–1857, husband of Mary), 50–52, 121
as grandfather of James Wishart, 122, 124
Spence, James, Sr. (1753–1795, Nestichio Batt's husband), 42–53
children of, 50–53
as HBC employee, 42–52
with Nestichio, 44–45, 46–50
Spence, Nestichio Batt. *See* Batt, Nestichio (1757–1827, Isaac's daughter, James Spence's wife)
St. John's Cathedral, Winnipeg (HBC cemetery), 74, 98
St. Paul's Parish, Red River Settlement, 130, 139, 203n11
St. Peter's Church (Indian cemetery), Manitoba, 98, 99, 129
St. Peter's Parish, Red River Settlement, 129, 199n28
Staynor, Thomas (Chief Factor), 49–50
steersmen, 44, 50
Stonechild, Blair, 147
Strange, General T.B., 152–53
Sutherland, Donna, 127–28, 184
Swampy Cree, 30

Thompson, David, 194n22
Thompson, John, 40
Tomison, William (Chief Factor), 40, 48–51, 56, 58, 169, 193n7
Treaty Six, 147
Tualatin Plains, Oregon, 97

United Church of Canada apology to Native people (1986), 209n1

Van Kirk, Sylvia, 63, 65, 75, 185
Vigar, Maude E. *See* Wishart, Maude E. Vigar (1876–1960, David Wishart's wife, Vern's grandmother)
Vrooman, Nicholas C.P., 156–57

Waiser, Bill, 147
Wandering Spirit, 148
Ward, John, 70
Williamson, Mary Dean Heller, 185

What Lies Behind the Picture?

Wilson, Clarendon
(Clarence), 160–61
Wishart family
  cultural heritage honours,
    164–70
  family reunion (1993), 22,
    176–77
  genealogy (chart), 24–25
  in Iowa, 122, 185, 203n17
  Orcadian fur traders,
    199n1–2
  research on family history, 8,
    15–16, 22–23, 182–85
  and their Native heritage,
    20–21, 170–82
Wishart, Aulta Woodall
(1904–1985, Vern's mother),
13, 21, 175
Wishart, Barbara Spence. *See*
Spence, Barbara (1800–1904,
wife of Thomas Wishart)
Wishart, Bill and Pat (Vern's
brother), 184
Wishart, David (1867–1956,
Maude's husband, also
Vern's grandfather)
  in Great Blizzard of 1887, 18,
    20
  and his Native heritage,
    20–21
  in Red Deer area, 22, 140–41,
    145–46
  in Rosebud area, 21, 167,
    174–75
Wishart, David (Vern's
nephew), 184–85
Wishart, Edward, 199n2
Wishart, Eliza Flett
(1835–1900, James' wife,
Vern's great-grandmother),
17, 125, 168
  children of, 140–42, 160–61,
    205n17
  cultural heritage honours,
    166, 166–69, 168
  in Great Blizzard of 1887, 16,
    18–20, 127
  and her medicine bag,
    127–30, 186n8
  and her Native heritage,
    20–21, 126, 129–30
  NW Rebellion of 1885 and,
    146–59
  in Red Deer area, 140–46,
    160–61, 164–67, 166
  in Red River Settlement,
    124–38
  in Rosebud area, 161–62
Wishart, Florence (Vern's
aunt), 174–75
Wishart, James (1830–1904,
Eliza's husband, also Vern's
great-grandfather), 17, 19,
168
  children of, 140–42, 160–61,
    205n17
  cultural heritage honours,
    166, 166–69, 168
  in Great Blizzard of 1887,
    16–20, 127

Index

and his Native heritage, 20–21, 126
impact of NW Rebellion of 1885 on, 146–59
in Red Deer area, 140–46, 160–61, 164–67, **166**
in Red River Settlement, 122–39
in Rosebud area, 160–62
Wishart, James (Vern's son), 182
Wishart, Jenny (daughter of James and Eliza), 160–61
Wishart, Johanna (Vern's wife), 182, 185, 226
Wishart, Mary and Herb (children of James and Eliza), 18
Wishart, Mary (daughter of Thomas and Barbara), 122
Wishart, Maude E. Vigar (1876–1960, David Wishart's wife, Vern's grandmother)
and her husband's Native heritage, 20–21
in Rosebud area, 21–22, 167, 174–75
Wishart, Nicholas, 102, 199n2
Wishart, Roy (1905–1959, Vern's father), 14
and his Native heritage, 13, 20–21, 181–82
with infant son Vern (photo), 13–15, **14**, 21
life of, 13–15, 167, 172, 174–75

Wishart, Shirley (1935– , Vern's sister)
cultural heritage honours, **168**, 168–71
"Eliza's Lament" (poem), 143–44
and her Native heritage, 20–23, 175–76
research on family history, 8, 15–16, 21, 22, 183–85
Wishart, Thomas (1797–1840, husband of Barbara Spence)
children of, 118–22, 124
as HBC employee, 102–3
in Iowa, 122, 185, 203n17
journey to Selkirk colony, 102–13
in Red River area, 117–22
as Selkirk Colony employee, 114–17
Wishart, Vernon R. (1927–), 14, **165, 226**
career as minister, 15, 22, 173–76, 209n1, 226
and his Native heritage, 13, 20–23, 172–82
as infant with father (photo), 13–15, **14**, 21
life of, 172–82, 226, **226**
research on family history, 8, 22, 177–80
Wishart Trail, Red Deer, 22, **165**
Wood, Kerry, 164–66

229

Woodall, Aulta. *See* Wishart, Aulta Woodall (1904–1985, Vern's mother)
Woolsey, Thomas, 87

York boats, 44, **57**, 65–67, 73, 87, 133
York Factory (HBC), 107
  history of, 30, 33, 37–38, 46, 49, 56, 106
  maps of routes from, **111, 116**
Young, Egerton Ryerson, 88

ABOUT THE AUTHOR

DR. VERNON R. WISHART was born in Alberta. He attended Colorado College in the United States on a hockey scholarship and returned to study for the ministry in the United Church at St. Stephen's College, Edmonton. In 1955 he went to Drew University in New Jersey on a travelling scholarship to do graduate work. It was there he met his wife, Johanna. They have five children and six grandchildren. After serving in northern, rural and urban communities, as well as in India, he retired in Edmonton. In his undergraduate and graduate studies, he majored in history. He has written extensively, and lectured at the University of Alberta and St. Stephen's College, from which he received an honorary doctorate.